FROM HERE TO MATURITY

About the Author

John A. Ishee has been affiliated with the Sunday School Board of the Southern Baptist Convention in various capacities for twelve years. He has been pastor and staff member in churches in Tennessee and Kentucky. He also has taught philosophy and psychology at Belmont College and The University of Tennessee in Nashville.

His broad academic training includes the Bachelor of Science Degree from Austin Peay State University, Clarksville, Tennessee; the Master of Religious Education Degree from Southern Baptist Seminary, Louisville, Kentucky; and the Master of Arts and Doctor of Education Degrees from George Peabody College in Nashville, Tennessee.

Other books by the author include *Is Christ for John Smith?* and *When Trouble Comes*, both published by Broadman Press.

Dr. Ishee, his wife, Myra, and son, Mark, live in Brentwood, Tennessee, a suburb of Nashville.

FROM HERE TO MATURITY

JOHN A. ISHEE

Broadman Press • Nashville, Tennessee

4282-39 (BRP)
4252-33 (Trade)
ISBN: 0-8054-5233-8 (Trade)

Dewey Decimal Classification: 248.4
Library of Congress Catalog Card Number: 75-2976
Printed in the United States of America

To
Myra and Mark,
of course!
They have helped me the most
in my Christian growth.

Preface

I guess I have been working on this book for forty years. That's how old I am. And there is a sense in which it is not yet complete. At least, I hope not. I want to grow some more, because my past growth has been gratifying.

What I have written represents where I am at this point in time. I have written with three basic assumptions in mind. First, the book is *confessional.* Much of my own pilgrimage of growth is described. I have occasionally used confessional elements to encourage the reader to reflect upon his own experiences as a means of growing in the Christian life. Also, I have shared portions of my own life because I would like for the reader to think of me as a fellow traveler on the pilgrimage of Christian growth.

Second, this book is intended to be *inspirational.* One of my primary purposes is to help the reader to become motivated toward being a growing person. While I have drawn heavily from ideas of numerous "scholars," I have sought to maintain simplicity in style and expression. Paul reminded us, "If you talk to a person in some language he doesn't understand, how will he know what you mean? You might as well be talking to an empty room" (1 Cor. 14:9, TLB).

Third, the book is intended to be *instructional.* The content and the structured experiences for personal and group use are designed to help the reader explore his growth as a Christian person.

I have a book in my personal library by Barry Stevens entitled *Don't Push the River (It Flows by Itself).* I like that title. It reminds me of something I never want to forget. Life is like a river. It flows until the end. We can't push time. We can't stop life. The river flows. But we can do a lot to determine how it flows and where it flows. That's what this book is about.

JOHN A. ISHEE

Brentwood, Tennessee

Contents

CHAPTER 1

GROWING: A Christian Life-style

Grow in spiritual strength and become better acquainted with our Lord and Savior Jesus Christ.

—2 Peter 3:18, TLB

You are Simon, John's son—but you shall be called Peter, the rock!

—John 1:42, TLB

Full many a flower is born to blush unseen
And waste its sweetness on the desert air.

—Thomas Gray

Consider the lilies of the field, how they grow

—Matthew 6:28

I want you to meet Lewis.

Lewis is eighty now. Recently the doctor told him that he had Parkinson's disease. But he is not bitter about it. Lewis has experienced fullness in life. He has been a player, not a spectator. He has played in the game of life; the grandstands were for someone else.

Lewis learned as a young man that he must be responsible for his life. Even though that load of responsibility has been heavy at times, he has never tried to give it away. Lewis has been a responsible, choosing person.

Lewis has many friends. I'm fortunate to be one of them. He helps his friends to grow as persons and in the process he experiences greater growth for himself. Lewis helped me "find myself" when I was beginning my career.

Lewis has a deep, abiding faith in God. He knows the God of the Bible. He experiences that God in daily prayer. He worships that God regularly in church.

Lewis is a giver. He gives of himself to help others. He has given himself to many worthwhile causes as a means of helping other people. Lewis gave part of himself to me. I'm a better person because Lewis gave.

What is Lewis going to do with the rest of his life? His goals are modest now, but he does have some. He always has. That is one of the reasons he has experienced fullness in life. In many ways, Lewis has experienced what Jesus referred to when he said, "I am come that they might have life, and that they might have it more abundantly" (John 10:10).

I also want you to meet Alice.

Alice is fifty years old and she feels that she has very little future. But that's not new. Alice has never felt that she had much future. She feels like life has passed her by. The reason she feels this way is because it really has. She watched it pass. She has been a spectator, not a player. She chose the security of the grandstand over the risk of playing the game.

Alice is an unhappy person. While she experiences times of pleasure, such times are like ocean waves that break upon the coastal rocks and diminish, rather than like a river that flows constantly, deep and wide.

Alice blames her disappointments on others—other people and other circumstances over which she feels that she has little control.

Alice has few friends, but deep inside she wishes she had more. She longs to know that someone really cares for her. Alice is a lonely person.

Alice is a troubled person. She is tense. She is anxious. She is fearful. Her mild depression, which she lives with most of the time, is only occasionally alleviated by the ocean waves of pleasure that break and diminish on the rocks of disappointment.

In reality, Alice is a selfish person. She has never really

given herself to any "great causes." She has always tried to get, not to give. She has wanted to hold on to what she has, not give it away. But she has lost at times. Alice is a poor loser.

Alice doesn't know much about God, only that which her tradition has passed along to her and the notions she has worked out from her life experiences. Alice has a Bible, but she doesn't read it. She doesn't go to church, because she doesn't like the people there. Alice prays occasionally, but most of her prayers are selfish prayers.

What is Alice going to do with the rest of her life? She doesn't know. She has no goals.

The choice is ours. If we are to experience the abundant life that Jesus promised, we must be growing persons. Failure to grow in the Christian life invites frustration, guilt, depression, and fear to rob us of the abundant life that Jesus came to give.

In the Sermon on the Mount, Jesus set a high goal for us. "You, therefore, must be perfect, as your heavenly Father is perfect" (Matt. 5:48). That word "perfect" means to be mature. And the Latin root of the word "mature" means "fully grown" or "ripe." Since we never come to the place in life where we are fully grown, the goal that Jesus set is never fully achieved. We never outgrow our need for growth. However, joy in life comes not in the full attainment of that goal, but through the efforts we put forth in trying to attain it.

In the play, *Shenandoah*, the author describes a scene that illustrates what I am saying about our growth in Christian personhood. Charlie Anderson, the father of the leading family in the play discovers that his youngest son has been taken prisoner by the Union armies. Immediately, he engages in a journey to find the lost son. Accompanied by other members of the family, he searches for the son for several weeks. His efforts are to no avail. Tired and frustrated, he holds a family conference in which his conversation goes something like this: "I knew from the start that there was little hope of finding the boy. But I just had to try. I hope all of you understand that. I just had to try!" A voice deep within us tells us that because of our finiteness we will never achieve the goal that Jesus set for us. At the same time, another voice tells us that we have to try. To fail to try is to miss the joy of Christian living.

Some people make few choices in life. They simply wander along with the tide of affairs, passive to life, missing the growth opportunities that they encounter each day. To such people, life is measured in a quantitative manner. Life consists of days, weeks, and years. The only punctuation marks in their lives are the exclamation marks that occur all too seldom and the nagging question marks that never seem to elicit enough interest and curiosity to lead them to find answers. In Shakespeare's words:

> To-morrow, and to-morrow, and to-morrow,
> Creeps on this petty pace from day to day
> To the last syllable of recorded time;
> And all our yesterdays have lighted fools
> The way to dusty death, Out, out brief candle!
> Life's but a walking shadow, a poor player
> That struts and frets his hour upon the stage
> And then is heard no more: it is a tale
> Told by an idiot, full of sound and fury,
> Signifying nothing.

There is another way to live that is far more exciting. It is a way of life that has meaning. It is a life characterized by growth. Specifically, it is a life characterized by Christian growth, for only the Christian has the potential of achieving growth as a person that results in satisfaction of his deeper needs.

I remember seeing an epitaph on a tombstone that read, "Born 1840—Died 1890—Lived 50 years." One could not help but wonder what the man did during those fifty years.

The fifth chapter of Genesis has often been called a "monument to mediocrity." Someone has referred to this chapter as a "genealogy of nobodies." The writer of Genesis moved at a rapid pace through the various generations. He used a formula to describe the lives of those he mentioned. His formula consisted of the idea that a person was born, lived a number of years, witnessed the birth of his children, and died. In the midst of all the monotony, there stands one shining exception. "Enoch walked with God" (Gen. 5:24). There was a difference in the life of Enoch and in the lives of those around him. Enoch saw life as a challenge. He walked with God each day in new and fresh experiences. He was one of the first people to experience what Lewis Sherrill has described as a pilgrimage. In the *Struggle of the Soul,* Sherrill describes life as a pilgrimage that "is consciously related not only to nature and humanity, but also to God who transcends nature and humanity." [1]

When a person becomes a Christian, growth is implied. Growth is the natural thing to do. However, it is not inevitable. A person must decide to grow. It takes effort. God gives the increase when this effort is put forth.

The goal is maturity. Maturity does not mean perfection. It means freedom—living freely with the free grace of God. There is freedom in the growing life, but a person realizes that freedom only as he assumes the responsibilities inherent in the growth process.

The Reasons for Growth

People sometimes seek security at the expense of happiness. When they find a comfortable niche in life, they begin to spend their energies defending that niche rather than continuing to grow. But the fruit of this approach has within it the seed of despair. Life is never static; it is constantly in process. The person who seeks to maintain the status quo misses the joy and challenge of living.

When a person "levels off" in life and is not growing, he becomes more susceptible to neuroses which rob him of meaning and fulfillment. Neuroses are mild (as compared to serious or chronic) mental and emotional disorders of personality that do not critically interfere with the normal functions of life. Nevertheless, they rob us of a feeling of self-worth and well-being, and block us in our reach toward our potential. Psychologist A. H. Maslow describes neurosis as "failure of personal growth." He states, "All the evidence that we have indicates that it is reasonable to assume in practically every human being, and certainly in almost every newborn baby, that there is an active will toward health, an impulse toward growth, or toward the actualization of human potential. But at once we are confronted with the very saddening realization that so few people make it." [2]

Neuroses place stress upon us and cause us to yearn for relief. Yet securing that relief is difficult because the neuroses cause us to possess a feeling that we are cut off from our own powers. Thus, we are caught in an uncomfortable and sometimes meaningless cycle. We are trapped.

How does a person break the cycle of nongrowth? How can he move off dead center and get his life moving again? The answer lies within a person's value system. A person must place priority upon his commitment to be a growing person.

A life-style of Christian growth involves commitment. It involves a concerted effort to make growth in personhood the organizing principle around which one builds his life. Commitment to a life-style of Christian growth is not only consistent with the will of God; it is also necessary for our personal well-being—as, indeed, the will of God always is.

When a person commits himself to a life-style of Christian growth, that commitment influences him to reorder his values and activities. Choices are made and time and energy are expended within the context of that basic commitment. For example, the person committed to a life-style of Christian growth chooses his vocation, his close friends, and how he will use his leisure to help him fulfill his basic commitment.

Christian growth as the center or organizing principle of life is often inconsistent with the values of our culture. Cultural values often focus on achievement or materialistic gain at the expense of personal development or growth. The person whose basic commitment is to materialistic gain orders his life around that commitment, often to the neglect of his well-being as a person. Moreover, because he fails to grow as a person, he is more vulnerable to neuroses—anxiety, depression, guilt—which rob him of the joys of life.

An outstanding difference between the commitment to growth and the commitment to gain is the location of these commitments in relation to the person. A commitment to gain is external to the person. It is "out there" and "other than" in its reference to the person. Consequently, it fails to nurture the person. I think that is what Jesus warned against when he said, "Take heed, and beware of covetousness: for a man's life consisteth not in the abundance of the things which he possesseth" (Luke 12:15). A basic commitment to gain which neglects growth is a "thirst never quenched," regardless of the success achieved in accumulating "things." John Steinbeck expressed this idea adequately in *The Grapes of Wrath* when he had one of his characters to state that if a person "needs a million acres to make him feel rich, and if he's poor in hisself, there ain't no million acres gonna make him feel rich, an' maybe he's disappointed that nothin' he can do'll make him feel rich."

In contrast, a life commitment to growth is internal. It nourishes the center of one's being, giving him purpose in life and strength in effort.

When Jesus and Nicodemus talked that night in Palestine long ago, they discussed eternal things. Jesus drew a parallel between physical birth and spiritual birth. "Truly, truly, I say to you, unless one is born of water and the Spirit, he cannot enter the kingdom of God" (John 3:5, RSV). "Born of water" referred to the process of physical birth. "Born of the Spirit" referred to spiritual birth.

The comparisons between physical growth and spiritual growth are also set forth in other places in the Bible. Paul wrote to the Christians at Corinth regarding their failure to grow in their spiritual lives. "But I, brethren, could not address you as spiritual men, but as men of the flesh, as babes in Christ. I fed you with milk, not solid food; for you were not ready" (1 Cor. 3:1-2, RSV). The reference to "babes in Christ" bears a striking similarity to the parallel Jesus used as he compared physical and spiritual birth.

Just as physical maturation is the normal process in life, it is normal and expected that the Christian will grow in his spiritual life. Just as the physical body must be nourished to maintain its process of development, the spiritual life must be fed. And the spiritual life can become unhealthy, just as the physical body can become unhealthy. Just as the absence of physical health results in unhappiness, lack of spiritual growth leaves the Christian frustrated with himself, alienated from other people, and guilt-ridden in his relationship to God.

One of the most encouraging examples of Christian growth is found in Simon Peter. Jesus invited Simon to follow him, saying: "You are Simon, the son of John? You shall be called Cephas (which means Peter)" (John 1:42, RSV). Winston Pearce captures the sheer improbability of Simon ever becoming the rock of which Jesus spoke.

> If there was one thing that Simon was not, it was a rock. Simon was not even a "kissing cousin" to a rock. Mercury, quick and hard to hold; Janus, looking both ways at once; Flanagan "on again, off again"; hot head, always "blowing his top"; profane, cursing, swearing; braggart, boasting, swaggering; stuttering, Satan tempting men, and even the Son of God, to be less than their best—any, all of these, you might have called Simon. But Cephas, Peter, a rock? That is the last name on earth that anyone would give Simon.[3]

Despite that improbability, Simon did become a rock. Follow his life through the New Testament. See him first thrust forth in growth, reach a plateau, and often shrink back from the pilgrimage. At Caesarea Philippi, note his bold assertion, "Thou art the Christ" (Mark 8:29). Follow him as he becomes a temptation to Jesus carrying out the will of God (Mark 8:29). Hear him declare that he will never deny his master (Matt. 26:35). Then pity him as he buries his face in his hands and weeps when he realizes that he indeed has denied the Master for self-preservation (Matt 26:75).

Is Simon finished? Has the hope of his becoming a rock completely diminished? Was Jesus wrong? Look further at the man. See him stand before a crowd, some of whom are hostile toward him, and witness for his Master (Acts 2:14 ff). Feel his pain as he is forced to break with tradition and preach the gospel to Cornelius, a Gentile (Acts 10:28). No, Jesus was not wrong. Simon came through. He became a rock. In a way, his admonition was autobiographical when he wrote, "But grow in grace, and in the knowledge of our Lord and Savior Jesus Christ" (2 Pet. 3:18).

The Process of Christian Growth

Christian growth does not always occur in a gradual and consistent pattern. More often it occurs in a pattern similar to physical maturation. As the child matures, he experiences times of rapid growth followed by times when growth is much slower in progress.

The poet Susan Coolidge described the process of Christian growth when she wrote:

> How does a soul grow? Not all in a minute
> Now it may lose ground, and now it may win it.
>
> ....
>
> Fed by discouragement, taught by disaster;
> So it goes forward, now slower, now faster.

Growth can occur as a person responds to both the positive and negative experiences of life. Certainly, those positive experiences of life help the person to grow in an uninhibited manner. In a sense, growth has its own reward. Growth comes from loving and being loved. Growth comes from the realization of a life goal. Growth comes from experiences that affirm us as persons of worth. However, some of the most growth-enhancing experiences can result from disappointments or tragic events in life. Such events often force a person to reevaluate his life and begin a new venture—a venture that would never have been started had not the difficult experience occurred. These difficult experiences may challenge a person who has become complacent in life.

Whether or not a difficult experience in life becomes an incentive for growth depends not so much on the event as the person's response to the event. Some people are crushed by difficulty; others, while feeling the pain of the experience, may be challenged to renewed efforts to grow. Edmund Vance Cooke reminds us:

> Oh, a trouble's a ton, or a trouble's an ounce,
> Or a trouble is what you make it.
> And it isn't the fact that you're hurt that
> counts,
> But only how did you take it?

On a windy March day, I was visiting Montgomery Bell State Park in Tennessee with an uncle who is a farmer. As we watched the tall trees sway from the impact of the wind, he commented, "Did you know that when the wind blows the tree, the roots of the tree are moved by the sway of the tree?" He went on to explain that the roots of the tree are cultivated in this manner. Thus, the wind helps a tree to sink its roots deeper into the soil so that it may continue to grow. Life is like that. The mighty tempests of life—tragedy, grief, disappointment—blow upon us. Yet these events can be a means of Christian growth. Instead of becoming embittered by these events, we can maintain our faith in God to take these events and use them as means by which we may grow. The crucifixion and resurrection of Jesus Christ are not only historical events, they are symbolic reminders of how God can take tragedy and bring about triumph. And it was "in the year that King Uzziah died" that Isaiah "saw also the Lord" (Isa. 6:1).

Perhaps the reason some people resist efforts at Christian growth is to avoid the pain that sometimes accompanies it. Reaching out for new experiences or having to face new experiences that are thrust upon us often results in insecurity or even grief. The growing person may feel insecure as he tries out new patterns of behavior. When a person explores new territory for his life, a feeling of insecurity is normal and usually inevitable. This feeling may tempt a person to abandon his quest. Jesus was faced with such a temptation as he spent forty days in the wilderness. His struggle involved whether or not he would take the familiar and expected path for his ministry or venture out into the new experience of fulfilling the will of God for his life. He chose the latter. His example serves as an inspiration to every Christian who is tempted to turn back from his commitment to Christian growth. He is our source of encouragement when we are tempted to shrink back into old patterns of behavior.

When a person experiences a loss, he feels grief. The extent of the grief depends on the extent to which the loss is felt. The sudden and unexpected loss of a loved one may result in acute grief. Other types of grief, less dramatic in nature, may not be so acutely felt. Growth, which involves reaching for new goals, also involves giving up old patterns of living. Until a person progresses far enough in his new growth venture to enjoy some measure of success, he may experience grief over giving up old and established patterns of living.

In spite of the insecurity and grief that a person may experience, the outcome of growth is always gratifying. A person who struggles to grow and experiences success deepens his faith in God as he becomes more acutely aware that God has been with him in his struggle. Moreover, the feelings accompanying achievement of growth goals are often rewards enough to assure the growing person that his efforts have not been in vain.

The Areas of Christian Growth

The biblical idea of Christian growth is an indisputable concept. Furthermore, the Bible is explicit in its description of the areas of Christian growth in one's life. What does Christian growth look like in everyday life? What are the areas of Christian growth? How do these areas relate to each other? The following chapters of this book seek to answer these questions. One assumption should be kept in mind: *Christian growth is maximized when understanding of God is balanced with understanding of oneself.*

Before proceeding to these chapters, I wish to preview the areas of Christian growth. Each of these areas will be discussed in succeeding chapters.

Growth in self-understanding.—A person is part of all he has experienced in his past and expects to experience in his future. In order to grow, he must understand how the forces of the past and the expectations of the future influence him in the present. He must face the responsibility for who he is in the present and who he will become in the future.

Growth in interpersonal relationships.—How a Christian relates to other people is an area of concern that cannot be ignored when Christian growth is considered. The growing Christian must constantly be seeking to make the "royal law of love" the basis for his relationships with other people. His Christian influence is dependent upon the extent to which he makes Christian love the hallmark of his relationships with other people.

Growth in self-awareness.—Self-awareness refers to a person's ability to recognize what is going on in his life in the present, particularly in terms of the emotions that he feels. Christians experience tension, fear, depression, guilt, and all the other emotions they experienced before they became Christians. Our commitment to Christ does not immune us from these emotions; it provides us with more resources to deal with them. How to handle these emotions constitutes an area of Christian growth that demands immediate and lifelong attention.

Growth through life's investments.—Jesus said that the person who loses his life will save it. Christian growth involves our willingness to give ourselves to worthy causes. The causes to which we give ourselves are investments that yield dividends in proportion to the amount invested.

Growth in relationship to God.—God is the source of growth. When we put forth the effort, he gives the increase. A person's understanding of God and how he experiences God in daily life is vital to Christian growth. When one considers the greatness of God, he is forced to admit that he never fully understands God. Therefore, his Christian life should be spent in growing in his understanding and experience with God.

Growth Is Goal-Oriented

Christian growth occurs best when a person puts forth efforts toward specific goals. When a person has in mind a goal that he desires to achieve, his efforts toward reaching that goal become purposeful. His priorities in terms of time and energy are influenced by this goal. Conversely, when a person has no goals, his growth lacks purpose.

In order to set worthy goals, a person must be convinced of the need for such goals in his life. George Bernard Shaw stated, "Some people see things as they are and ask 'why?'; I see things that never have been and ask 'why not?' " Such a vision is needed by all Christians. Since Christian growth is a never ending process, the Christian must be constantly striving to reach new heights in his Christian pilgrimage. He must be continously assessing his character, motives, devotion, and depth of service. Out of these assessments, new goals will emerge.

The areas of growth may be illustrated graphically by the "Christian Growth Model." Note that the arrows on the diagram point not only to the areas of growth, but also

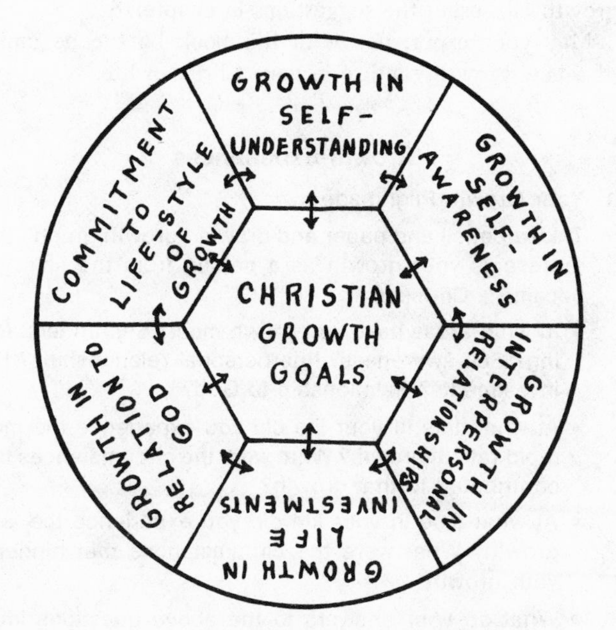

CHRISTIAN GROWTH MODEL

to the interrelationships of the various areas. Thus, Christian growth is a dynamic process in which a person is growing not only in one area, but in several. These areas are integrated toward the achievement of specific growth goals.

* * *

I encourage you to read the following chapters in a slow, reflective manner. Bring your own perceptions freely into the process of reading. Examine where you are in relation to the concepts set forth. Complete the "Growth Experiences" at the end of each chapter. You may wish to join with other persons in your church or community in a group growth lab, using the suggestions in chapter 8.

May your experience with this book be the beginning of a new growth venture in your Christian life.

Growth Experiences

1. Your Growth Pilgrimage

   Take a pencil and paper and draw a "growth graph" that represents your growth as a person from the time you became a Christian.

   - In what areas have you grown most? Self-understanding? Self-awareness? Interpersonal relationships? Life investments? Relationship to God?
   - At what time in your life did you experience the most rapid rate of growth? What were the circumstances that contributed to that growth?
   - At what time in your life did you experience the least growth? What were the circumstances that hindered your growth?
   - What do your answers to the above questions imply about what you should do to aid your growth as a Christian person?

2. Value Assessment

Reflect on your interests and activities for the past month.

- How much time and energy have you spent on "gain" goals?
- How much time and energy have you spent on "growth" goals?
- What does the way you spend your time and energy tell you about your primary values? Are you pleased with these values? Begin to think about how you should alter your life-style to achieve a greater degree of growth as a Christian person.

CHAPTER 2

REFLECTING: Know Thyself

The trouble, dear Brutus, is not in our stars, but in ourselves.

—*Shakespeare*

Know then thyself, presume not God to scan;
The proper study of mankind is man.

—*Alexander Pope*

The unexamined life is not worth living.

—*Socrates*

And . . . he came to himself.

—*Luke 15:17*

Of all of God's creation, only the human being has the capacity to reflect upon his existence. A person can reflect upon his past, examine his present, and project hopes for the future. This ability to examine one's existence carries with it the implicit responsibility to do so. It is a responsibility not to be taken lightly. Sometimes it involves discomfort. Perhaps Walt Whitman was feeling the weight of this responsibility when he wrote:

> I think I could turn and live with animals . . .
> They do not sweat and whine over their condition;
> They do not lie awake in the dark and weep
> for their sins . . .

The psalmist was reflecting upon his existence when he wrote:

> When I consider thy heavens, the works of thy fingers, the moon and the stars which thou hast ordained, What is man that thou art mindful of him? And the son of man that thou visiteth him? For thou hast made him a little lower than the angels, and

has crowned him with glory and honor (Ps. 8:3-5).

The Greek philosopher, Socrates, reminded us that "The unexamined life is not worth living." Conversely, the person who is willing to examine his life can find untapped resources to help him reach toward his potential as a person.

All of us are aware of our existence. It is impossible to live and breathe without being aware that we take up space in the world. However, it is unfortunate that many people never try to go beyond the awareness of their existence to discover the meaning of their existence and the extent to which they are reaching toward the potential that God has placed within them.

The Purpose of Self-Examination

Edgar Guest in his poem "Myself" expressed one of the purposes of self-examination when he wrote:

> I have to live with myself, and so
> I want to be fit for myself to know
> ....
> I don't want to stand, with the setting sun
> And hate myself for the things I've done

The purpose of self-examination is not to become paralyzed by introspection. Albert McClellan in his book *Openness and Freedom* states that the first step toward openness toward oneself is the willingness to look within. Then he reminds us of an important second step: *the willingness not to look too long!* It is possible for a person to become so conscious of self that he fears his actions and loses his spontaneity. While a person can benefit from "standing outside himself" and examining his life, it is also possible to become "locked inside himself" to the extent that he becomes immobilized.

The purpose of self-examination is to become aware of

one's strengths and weaknesses. As a person examines his life, he often discovers assets of which he was unaware. The sculptor, Michelangelo, looked upon a crude piece of marble and remarked, "There's an angel in that piece of marble and I want to set him free." Buried within many people are gifts and talents that they do not know about. Thomas Gray was correct when he stated:

> Full many a flower is born to blush unseen
> And waste its sweetness on the desert air.

Through self-examination, a person can begin to discover these gifts and put them to use in beneficial ways.

Another purpose of self-examination is to discover areas of life where improvements are needed, areas that in many cases block a person from reaching his potential. If the idea of discovering weaknesses is disturbing, we may be encouraged by realizing that every person possesses both strengths and weaknesses. Our self-examination does not create these weaknesses; it merely uncovers them and places us in a position to begin to deal with them in a constructive manner.

Self examination is no easy task. Rollo May, in *Man's Search for Himself*, has reminded us that many people today find it almost impossible to realize that the Greek philosopher's precept "Know thyself" was a call for the individual to engage in the most difficult challenge of all. Soren Kierkegaard expressed the challenge adequately when he said, "To venture in the highest sense is precisely to become aware of one's self."

The greater the insight we possess into our natures and motives, the more we can begin to control our lives. From the outset we must admit that we will never become completely aware of ourselves. There always will be "blind spots" as we look at ourselves. However, we can learn more about ourselves. And we can commit ourselves to a lifetime of effort to come to a greater understanding of our strengths and weaknesses.

The Path of Self-Examination

The person who takes seriously the challenge of self-examination must consider in various ways his past and his expectations of the future in regard to how they influence him in the present.

Each person's gallery of memories contains joys and sorrows, love and hate, blessings and curses. But the past should not victimize us; it should be a school of memories from which we learn to better understand ourselves. Paul wrote, "When I was a child, I spake as a child, I understood as a child, I thought as a child: but when I became a man, I put away childish things" (1 Cor. 13:11).

In examining the past, a person has two alternatives. First, he can use the past as an alibi for remaining as he is in the present. Secondly, he can learn from the past, rather than being victimized by it.

People who use their past as a resource for personal growth usually experience what philosophers and psychologists call "existential moments." Existential moments are times when a person becomes acutely aware that he exists not only in relation to other people or events, but also separate and apart from other people and events. He realizes that he must assume responsibility for his being; he can no longer blame past or present external circumstance for who he is. "To be or not to be? That is the question." He realizes that while his past is always with him, he can no longer use it as a "cop out" for the responsibilities of living in the present.

In a meeting I conducted several months ago, a group of people were examining their past. I had asked them to share with each other their answers to four questions. (1) How would you describe the house in which you lived from ages seven to thirteen? (2) How was your home heated? (3) What was the "warm spot" in your home in terms of affection? and (4) At what time in your life did God become more than just a word? One young man in the group shared his answer and it went something like this:

> The only love I remember receiving when I was a child was the love of a Collie dog. That dog meant a lot to me. One day when I went to the mailbox, which was about a half-mile down the road, a farmer came down the road driving a piece of farm machinery. My dog began to chase the farm machinery, as dogs often do. I watched as the farmer swerved the machinery, trying to hit the dog. On the third try, he ran over my dog, crushing his pelvic bone. The dog pulled himself into the tall grass beside the road. I went over where he was and sat there and cried for what seemed like a long time. Then I went back to the house and got some water. I also got my rifle. I went back to where the dog lay, gave him some water, then sat there and cried some more. Then I heard the farm machinery coming back up the road. I heard it stop and watched the driver as he pushed back the tall grass, searching for the dog. Before he realized it, he had walked upon the site where we sat and my rifle was pointed directly between his eyes about six inches from his head. . . .

The young man began to cry as he stated, "I have never wanted to kill a person except then. But I did want to kill that person." After a period of silence, I asked, "Why did you not kill him, Bob?" His reply demonstrated that he had already begun to learn from his past, rather than being victimized by it. "I realized," he said, "that all the hostility I felt in that moment was not his fault. I felt that way because there had been an absence of love in my life."

After speaking to a group of men on the importance of self-examination, I was approached by a man who commented, "It was not until about a year ago that I really began to feel alive. When I was fourteen, I accidentally killed my brother in a hunting accident. But about a year ago a group of friends helped me to surface and begin to deal with the guilt I had carried for twenty years." With a smile of hope he commented, "I'm not out of the woods yet, but I'm on my way. At least, I feel more alive."

On another occasion as I counseled with a young man, he stated that on three occasions he almost became a Christian. He really wanted to believe, but something was holding him back. As we talked, he told me that when he was an infant his father had deserted his mother. I asked, "If your father told you that he would do something, would you believe it? "No," he replied, "my father never kept his word." As we continued to talk, he came to realize that his lack of ability to trust God grew out of his lack of ability to trust his father. Once he realized this, he was able to break through the barrier that had prevented him from expressing genuine faith.

These stories illustrate the results that can occur when a person examines his past and learns from it. The fact that a person's past may not contain events as dramatic as these in no way minimizes the extent of learning that can occur.

We can learn not only from the tragedies of the past but also from the joys and fond memories. Our pasts hand us not only problems to conquer but also joys to embrace. Many of us are like Timothy, to whom Paul wrote, "I call to remembrance the unfeigned faith that is in thee, which dwelt first in thy grandmother Lois, and thy mother Eunice; and I am persuaded that is in thee also" (2 Tim. 1:5). In examining our past, we can call to remembrance those positive experiences we had as we grew up. Thus, we can balance the negative with the positive, tragedy with joy, our noble heritage with our painful memories.

The writer of Proverbs stated that "Where there is no vision, the people perish" (Prov. 29:18). It was his way of saying that an essential ingredient for a growing life is hope for the future. Just as the legacies of the past influence the present, our hopes for the future do also. We live on two levels—the public level which is our doing and the private level, the thinking level and rehearsing level, where we prepare for future roles we want to play. As a person reflects on his future, he anticipates how he will live and the nature of his existence. He may even imagine how long he will live and how he will die.

In *Scripts People Live,* Claude Steiner sets forth the notion that each person lives his life according to a predetermined life script which the person has either consciously or unconsciously constructed. At times the person may not be aware of the existence of the script. Nevertheless, the script is present and influences behavior each day. Decisions are made, actions are taken, and feelings are affected by the life script that the person possesses. To the extent that the life script is not consciously examined, it may serve as a victimizing force in a person's life. In other words, a person can become victimized by his concept of the future, just as he can be victimized by the legacies of the past.

In many cases, a person's life script becomes a self-fulfilling prophecy, not because a life script has some magical quality but because a person acts in a way that causes the life script to become reality. If a person does not expect to achieve a particular goal or result in the future, his lack of expectancy bears a strong influence upon his ability to achieve it. Thus, it is possible for us to limit our potential by the way we view the future. Examining how one views the future can help him bring into sharper focus his life script, examine it, and alter it as he would like for it to be.

Admittedly, a person's life script does not always prove valid. Circumstances may occur that are in stark contrast to the life script. Whether or not they are valid or come true is not the primary point. The primary point is that a life script influences how a person lives in the present. The less that life script is examined, the greater are the possibilities that a person may become victimized by it.

Just as a person can retreat into the past as a means of escaping the responsibilities of the present, he can also take flight into the future and neglect the present. He may, when facing some problem in the present, remind himself that things will be better "When I get married," or "When I graduate from college," or "When I get another job." In other words, instead of possessing healthy hope for the future, he projects unrealistic hopes upon the future as a means of escaping the responsibilities of the present.

But hope for the future should not be a means of escape. Rather, hope for the future should be an energizing force that contributes to a person's well-being.

The past and future always influence the present. Therefore, rather than sequencing time as past, present, and future, which is chronological time, a more appropriate way may be to sequence time as past, future, and present. Such a sequence is experiential time, for it focuses on the present. It is in the present that we live. We have no other option. Therefore, how we deal with the present becomes crucial as it relates to our legacy of the past and our hopes for the future. On a sundial at the entrance to Johns Hopkins Hospital in Baltimore there is an inscription which reads:

The only hour within thy hand
Is the hour on which the shadow stands.

Jesus beckoned us to "Take no thought of the morrow: for the morrow shall take thought for the things of itself. Sufficient unto the day is the evil thereof" (Matt. 6:34). The only segment of time in which one can act is the present moment. Seeking to escape into the past or future encourages a person to fail to assume the responsibilities of the present.

As a person seeks to live in the present, he must give attention to the extent to which he is willing to seek autonomy over the external circumstances of his environment. He must examine his willingness to be a responsible person in assuming control over his life. An oversimplified way to approach the control factor is to divide people into two categories: radar people and gyroscope people.[1] Radar people are people who allow external circumstances to have the larger degree of control over their lives. A radar set is designed to *detect* and respond to objects that come within its area of scanning. What the radar reflects depends on what comes into its domain of detection. Radar people are people who seek to have little control over forces around them. They simply reflect the attitudes, beliefs, and behavior of people around them, giving little attention to discriminating between what they should or should not do. Since they receive their sense of direction from persons and objects external to themselves, they spend a great deal of time seeking to keep up with what is going on around them, picking up the signals they should reflect. They may or may not like people, but they do *need* people. They usually appear to be friendly people, because an outgoing nature is a means of keeping the radar set in focus.

Radar people often lack the necessary degree of identity.

They exist too much in relation to others and not enough in relation to self. Lacking inner convictions, they often find themselves experiencing inner conflict as they encounter conflicting values in the people around them. Moreover, radar people sometimes are troubled and anxious people because their need for approval by other people is not always met, resulting in feelings of rejection and depression.

Gyroscope people are people who possess a sense of inner directiveness. In contrast to a radar set, a gyroscope is a *directional* instrument, rather than a *detection* instrument. Gyroscope people are people who, while not oblivious or indifferent to external influences, seek to maintain control over their lives.

The gyroscope person accepts willingly the responsibility for who he is and what he does. Life for him involves making choices and being responsible for those choices. His choices center around three main concerns. First, he is concerned with his identity. The basic question is "Who am I?" His efforts are directed toward establishing himself as a person in his own right. Second, the gyroscope person is concerned with his relationship to his external environment. "What am I a part of?" is the basic question at hand. Thus, he frequently asks himself if he is satisfied with the world to which he is connected. Finally, the gyroscope person gives attention to the matter of controlling his life. "To what extent am I controlling my life? To what extent is it being controlled by others? How do I feel about those controls?" While the gyroscope person is never free from external controls and may not even wish to be, he is aware of those controls and how he feels about them.

When I speak of the matter of control over one's life, there comes the inevitable question about the lordship of Christ. Basically, the question is, "Is it wrong to want to control our lives?" The members of my Sunday School class were discussing freedom and responsibility. One class member commented, "Through life's experiences, I came to realize that I must assume control and responsibility for my life." Another class member replied, "But if you belong to the Lord, how can you say "I must assume control of my life?" The first member replied, "I came to the point in life where I realized that unless I had control of my life, I really could not give it to the Lord."

In order to give oneself to the Lord, one must first take hold of his life. He must not allow the external forces of the culture to control him. The forces that would exert control on our lives are many. Some people are controlled by the compulsion to be accepted. To these people, not rejection, but the fear of rejection controls their actions. They do not control their lives. Rather they are controlled by the compulsion to be accepted. Their temptation is not unlike the temptation that Jesus faced. Rather than resisting the temptation, however, they yield to it. They would be willing to turn stones into bread if it would increase their acceptance by people.

Inevitably, there comes a time when a person is faced with the option of either being controlled by external forces or being responsible for who he is and who he becomes. It is when he accepts this responsibility that he can begin to live freely within the free grace of God. It is then that he can fully give himself to the Lord. Perhaps that is why Jesus said, "If any man come to me, and hate not his father, and mother, and wife, and children, and brethren, and sisters, yea, and his own life also, he cannot be my disciple. And whosoever does not bear his cross, and come after me, cannot be my disciple" (Luke 14:26-27).

The Goal of Self-Examination

Why all this attention to self-examination? What is the purpose? The goal is to arrive at an adequate self-concept, to come to terms with self, to accept oneself as a person of worth who is grateful for his strengths and willing to accept his weaknesses.

In *The Spirit of St. Louis*, the late Charles Lindbergh made an interesting observation about his flight to Paris. He pointed out the dangers in his transatlantic flight of flying either too high or too low. There was an optimum altitude that was within the range of safety. If the plane had flown too high, the wings would have become iced and the pilot would have lost control of the plane. If it had flown too low, a sudden heavy fog might have caused the plane to experience a quick dip in altitude, thus sending it into the ocean. So the pilot had to exercise caution in not flying too high or too low.

A healthy self-concept is like that. In Romans, Paul wrote that a person ought not to think too highly of himself, but ought to possess a sober appraisal of his worth (see Rom. 12:3). In another place he said we should not be wise in our own conceit (see Rom. 12:6).

What is the biblical teaching regarding one's self-concept? How is the Christian to think of himself? On the one hand, he faces the reality that he is a sinner. Like Adam, he has rebelled against the authority and will of God. On the other hand, he is aware that he is created in the image of God. However, the presence of sin in his life should not overshadow his awareness that he is created in the image of God. It is because of the coexistence of sin and God's image within him that he, like Walt Whitman, may "lie awake in the dark and weep for our sins."

The full revelation of the gospel puts sin in proper perspective. Jesus said, "Ye shall know the truth, and the truth shall set you free" (John 8:32). Jesus took upon himself our sins. Thus, there is the promise that "If we confess our sins, he is faithful and just to forgive us our sins, and cleanse us from all unrighteousness" (1 John 1:9).

I believe there are three things a Christian should never do. First, he should never leave Jesus hanging on the cross. He should get him into the tomb and up on the third day. Second, he should never leave the prodigal son in the pigsty. He ought to get the boy home, back to a forgiving father. Finally, he should not allow sin to blind him from the reality of God's forgiveness, because that forgiveness is essential for a healthy self-concept—and a healthy self-concept is essential to his growth as a Christian person.

It is possible to "wallow in unworthiness" to the extent that a person impairs the realization of his potential. It is also possible to possess such an exalted self-concept that he blinds himself to reality and robs himself of growth potential. Between these two extremes lies the biblical concept of how a person should think of himself.

Because he is created in the image of God, every person is a person of worth. However, the person may not feel that he has worth. But God has created us with the potential to possess a worthy self-concept.

Sin is a destructive force to the self-concept. It not only alienates a person from God, but it also alienates a person from his better self, from his potential. One has only to consider the life of the first man to realize that sin is a destructive force to the self-concept. There is no evidence that Adam had any impediments to a worthy self-concept prior to his yielding to temptation. He had unimpaired fellowship with God and wholesome interpersonal relationships. Moreover, he did not experience shame, guilt, anxiety, or any of the other feelings that hinder a healthy self-concept. However, when sin entered his life, these destructive forces became a reality. Adam felt cut off from God and troubled with himself. The wages of sin is death, and Adam began to die a little when he first experienced sin. Part of what began to die was the adequate and worthy view that man possessed regarding himself. The presence of sin with its accompanying anxiety, guilt, and hostility influenced him to feel that he was an inadequate being. That is still true today.

God can work in a person's life to help him overcome his feelings of inadequacy. It happens as the person experiences God's forgiveness and learns to live out the love relationships of the gospel.

Jesus said that the greatest commandment was to love God. The second commandment was to love others as we love ourselves. The love of self is essential to loving other people. Kierkegaard appropriately stated it in this manner:

> If anyone will not learn from Christianity to love himself in the right way, then neither can he love his neighbor. . . . To love one's self in the right way and to love one's neighbor are absolutely analogous concepts, are at the bottom one and the same. . . . Hence the law is: "You shall love yourself as you love your neighbor when you love him as yourself." [2]

A feeling of worthwhileness cannot exist to the greatest extent apart from love that is given and received.

Because some people find it difficult to perceive of themselves as persons of worth, they invent substitutes for self-worth. These substitutes actually are defense mechanisms to conceal from themselves and others the low regard that they have of themselves.

One way that a person may seek a feeling of self-worth is by engaging in an inordinate number of activities. Their rationale is "I must be important; look at all the things I am doing. The vast array of activities is an attempt to drown an inadequate concept of self. Often such people are like the person described in *Canterbury Tales*, of whom Chaucer wrote, "Methinks he seemed busier than he was." "To be idle," wrote Robert Louis Stevenson, "requires a strong sense of personal identity."

Another substitute for self-worth is self-exaggeration. Persons with inadequate self-concepts often feel they must "sell" themselves to other people. Like the Pharisees, they parade their "good deeds" before men. Furthermore, they may be sensitive to criticism or any innuendo that suggests that they are not highly regarded by others. Their self-concept is a shell, firm on the surface but hollow inside. As T. S. Eliot stated, they are:

> . . . hollow men
> Shape without form, shade without colour.

Such persons are often referred to by their peers as conceited. Actually, the conceit is an attempt to hide a low feeling of self-worth.

Self-contempt, while on the surface appears to be the opposite of self-worth, is another substitute for self-worth. People who possess a low regard for themselves often engage in self-contempt as a means of drowning their feelings of inadequacy. Such self-contempt provides a person with a reason for self-hate, a reason he needs because he is not entirely capable of self-love.

Erich Fromm provides an excellent discrimination between selfishness and self-love. He points out that self-love is not the same as selfishness; it is the opposite of it. The person who lacks an adequate feeling of self-worth may engage in excessive self-concern, which is selfishness. On the other hand, the person who has a sound love for self has the capacity to love others, rather than being consumed by self-concern.

* * *

If a person is to begin to know himself, he must examine his past, asking, "What does it teach me about myself?" He must examine his hopes for the future, asking, "What do they teach me about my life in the present?" He must examine how he assumes the responsibility for his being in the present. Finally, he must arrive at a view of himself which enables him to truthfully say, "I am not all I can be or should be, but I like what I see in myself at this point in time." When a person has arrived at this point, he can go on toward the achievement of the potential that God is willing to give him.

Growth Experiences

1. The Past

   List the three most disappointing and tragic events you have experienced. Then list the three most gratifying experiences you have had. How have they influenced you in terms of

   - What you like and dislike?
   - What you are willing to try or afraid to try?
   - How you feel about yourself?

   In what ways are these events continuing to influence your behavior? Are these influences helping or hindering your Christian growth?

2. The Future

   Attempt to surface your life script. Write down answers to the following questions.

- How many years do you expect to live?
- What are some goals you wish to achieve before you die?
- What are your greatest fears of the future?
- In what ways are the answers to the above questions influencing your life?

3. Your Present
   - To what extent do you feel that you can shape your future?
   - To what extent do you feel that other people control your life against your will?
   - What factors in your life help or hinder you from assuming responsibility for who you are and what you do?
4. About Yourself
   - Draw a horizontal line across a sheet of paper. Number points on the line from 1 to 10, giving approximately even space between each number. With 1 representing a low self-concept and 10 representing a high self-concept, circle the number that best represents how you feel about yourself. Why do you rate yourself as you do? When do you like yourself the most? the least?
5. Feedback
   - Your self-understanding can be increased as you share your deep thoughts with others.
   - Share at appropriate times with other people some of the outstanding memories of your past and your hopes for the future.
   - Ask other persons to give you honest feedback on how they perceive you as a person. Act responsibly on this information, deciding whether or not you consider it valid. If you do not consider it valid, seek to discover why other persons perceive you as they do.

CHAPTER 3

CARING: For Whom the Bell Tolls

No man is an island. . . .

Therefore, never ask for whom the bell tolls; it tolls for thee.

—*John Donne*

In the sense in which a man can ever be said to be at home in the world, he is at home not through dominating, or explaining, or appreciating, but through caring and being cared for.

—*Milton Mayeroff*

This is my commandment, That you love one another, as I have loved you.

—*John 15:12*

Margaret Craven, in her tender, moving novel, *I Heard the Owl Call My Name,* tells the story of a young man who had only a short time to live. The young man is vicar in the church. The story begins with a conversation between the young man's doctor and the Bishop who is charged with responsibility to assign the young vicar to his place of service for the church.

The doctor said to the Bishop, "So you see, my lord, your young ordinand can live no more than three years and doesn't know it. Will you tell him, and what will you do with him?"

The Bishop said to the doctor, "Yes, I'll tell him, but not yet. If I tell him now, he'll try too hard. How much time has he for an active life?

"A little less than two years if he's lucky."

So short a time to learn so much? "It leaves me no choice; I shall send him to my hardest parish . . ."

"Then I hope you'll pray for him, my lord."

But the Bishop only answered gently that it was where he would wish to go if he were young again. . . .[1]

The Bishop related to the young priest in a way that aided his growth. Behind the story is the assumption that there is so much gratification in the growing life that a person should not be prohibited from that growth, even if he has only a short time to live.

Each time one life touches another, the event is crucial. The event may be casual or coincidental, but it is still crucial. It is crucial because each relationship we have is filled with potential for growth.

Recently a friend told me about a decision his son had made. His son sat down and listed all the people with whom he associated. Then he pondered the list, asking two questions: "Am I contributing to this person's growth?" and "Is this person contributing to my growth?" Those names that received a yes to either question were kept on the list. Those names that received a no to both questions were taken off. The son had concluded that the primary purpose of relationships was to facilitate the growth of one or both parties. He concluded that he would no longer initiate relationships with persons who contributed nothing to his growth. However, he also concluded that should any of these people initiate contact with him, he would be open to the contact. Perhaps the other person's initiative in the relationship would be a signal that he was wrong in his assessment of his contribution to the other person's life.

All of us have in our gallery of memories and in our present environment persons who help us to actualize the potential that is within us. As Kierkegaard has beautifully stated, these people help us "to be that self which one truly is."

When a person relates to another person in a way that helps the other person to grow, he, in the process, achieves growth for himself. On numerous occasions when I have led conferences in human relationships, the persons in the conference have not only spoken to me but also have spoken for me when they have expressed how the experience has contributed to their growth as persons. Carl Rogers expressed this concept when he stated: "The degree to which I can create relationships which facilitate the growth of others as separate persons is a measure of the growth I have achieved in myself."

The Caring Relationship

It was New Year's Eve. As interim pastor of the church, I had announced on the previous Sunday that Wednesday night prayer service would be a time of sharing. I requested that each person bring with him one object that symbolized a spiritually significant event that had occurred in his life during the past year. Of all the objects that were brought, most of them symbolized an event that related to caring. One teenager brought a plane ticket from New York to Nashville. She stated, "When I came to Nashville, I found Christ, who cares for me, and I found a caring church." A mother shared a note that her young son had hidden under his pillow. The note said, "Mommy, I love you." A young lady who was having marital difficulties shared a card she had received from her Sunday School teacher. She wept as she said, "When I received this card, it was the only expression of care I had received in months."

The growing person is a caring person. His caring helps other people to grow. In the process, he himself grows. "In the sense in which a man can ever be said to be at home in the world, he is at home not through dominating, or explaining, or appreciating, but through caring and being cared for." [2]

There is a sense in which a society can evaluate its values by the number of words it has that mean essentially the same thing. Consider, for example, the number of words or phrases our society uses to refer to the automobile. The auto makers have added a lot of words to our vocabulary. Their efforts have succeeded because we value the automobile. It is an essential and valuable part of our way of life. Norman Greenburg, an anthropologist at Western Michigan University, reminds us that the Eskimos use numerous words to refer to ice. Ice is an integral experience in their lives, so they have invented a lot of words to refer to it.

There is also a sense in which the word "caring" is synonymous with "loving." Yet the parallel does not always hold. I chose to refer to relationships that foster growth as caring relationships, rather than loving relationships because the word "love" in the English language is subject to and often is the object of misuse. Instead of having numerous words to refer to one type of love, we have one word that refers to love of varying kinds and degrees. For example, we "love" apple pie, football games, our children, our spouses, our country, and God. One word—love—is the verb that we use to try to describe this web of relationships. Maslow stated, "I have had to make up . . . words because the English language is rotten for good people. It has no decent vocabulary for the virtues. Even the nice words get all smeared up—'love,' for instance." [3]

The biblical word that is used predominantly to describe the love of God toward us and that love which Christians are to have for others is *agape.*

Agape is the word the Bible uses when it says, "God so loved the world that he gave . . ." (John 3:16). That is what Jesus was talking about when he said to love your neighbor as yourself. It starts with love for oneself. Then it reaches out to a compassionate love for other people.

Read 1 Corinthians 13:4-7 from *The Living Bible, Para-*

phrased. Notice some of the characteristics of *agape* that are mentioned there. This is the way a person acts when he begins to show other people that he really cares for them.

> Love is very patient and kind, never jealous or envious, never boastful or proud, never haughty or selfish or rude. Love does not demand its own way. It is not irritable or touchy. It does not hold grudges and will hardly even notice when others do it wrong. It is never glad about injustice, but rejoices whenever truth wins out. If you love someone you will be loyal to them no matter what the cost. You will always expect the best of him, and always stand your ground in defending him.

Agape is spontaneous and unmotivated. It exists as an integral part of the person's being. This love can be expressed not only to people who agree with us, but also people with whom we have differences. Since its reason for being is not in the object of love but in the initiation of love, it can "weather the storms" of conflict and not disappear. *Agape* can "turn the other cheek" and "go the second mile" because its reason for being is not dependent on the external circumstances that confront and challenge it.

Agape is synonymous with caring. *Caring for people and relating to them in a way that facilitates growth means that I become a part of someone else's life and, at the same time, allows that person to exist apart from me in his own right.* When we seek to create such relationships, we are continuing in the act of creation that God began. He created man to be a part of him, yet he created man as a person free to choose, separate from him and existing in his own right.

Substitutes for Caring

The opposite of caring is not always lack of caring. More often it is subtle deviation of caring which may have the same effects of explicit lack of care. The factor that makes these substitutes for caring so difficult to deal with is their existence under the guise of caring. Often these substitutes for caring meet only one part of the definition of caring stated above. Namely, a person becomes a part of someone else's life but fails to let the other person exist separate from him in his own right.

One type of relationship that sometimes exists under the guise of caring is *parasitic attachment.* One person attaches himself to another in a dependency role. One person becomes the hero or rescuer; the other person becomes the person being rescued. Such a relationship fails to foster growth in either party. The rescuer receives nothing from the relationship, with the possible exception of gratification of his ego. The "person in distress" receives reinforcement for his dependency role, thus failing to develop the confidence and skills essential for self-direction.

Overprotection, another substitute for caring, is in many ways like parasitic attachment, with one exception. The relationship is initiated and maintained by the "rescuer," rather than the "person in distress."

The overprotected person is deprived of the opportunity to grow because he is discouraged from venturing out. He is not allowed to struggle with life's problems; thus, he never learns how to deal with them adequately.

The person who initiates or maintains a relationship of overprotection is actually expressing a lack of confidence in the person he is protecting. How can an expression of lack of confidence in the person be interpreted as caring? The overprotective person is often protecting himself as much or more than he is protecting the other person. He may be protecting himself from the embarrassment or shame he would feel if the other person made a noticeable mistake.

Parents are easy prey for the overprotective relationship. Under the guise of caring, they may deprive their children of opportunities to grow in self-confidence by doing too much for them or sheltering them from the inevitable pain that accompanies responsibility.

On one occasion, I interviewed James L. Sullivan, former president of the Southern Baptist Sunday School Board, about the type of home from which he came. His words express succinctly and explicitly the opposite of overprotection and the essence of caring that his parents provided for the children in the family. He stated:

> All through the years, my parents let us struggle through our own problems. They would help us in any way, but they would not jump in prematurely and answer things for us. They let us work out our own problems because they knew that convictions are developed in this manner. They assured us of their interest, prayers, and support. But they let us solve our own problems. Then they backed us in our own decisions.[4]

Overprotection is by no means limited to parent-child relationships. It is often expressed in husband-wife relationships. At times it is expressed between employer and employee. On occasions it is expressed between friends. But in most cases, overprotection does not express caring; it expresses lack of confidence, which may be interpreted as lack of caring.

The opposite of expressing care for a person is the *manipulation* of that person to satisfy one's own needs. The manipulator often seeks to relate to other persons in a way that communicates that he cares, but in reality his "caring" is only a front to overcome the other person's resistance to his manipulation. Thus, the manipulator has a hidden agenda. He reasons, "If I can make the other person believe that

I really care for him, I can use that belief as a basis for getting the person to do what I want. Manipulation is often subtle. Sometimes it is unconscious. The manipulator may not have examined his motives and when confronted with his manipulative manner will at first deny it. However, his denial of it makes it no less real.

Another technique of the manipulator is the use of guilt. If the manipulator can get the other person to agree with him on goals he deems worthy, he can then heap guilt on the other person if the person does not enter into his efforts to reach the goals.

The intent of the manipulator is not to help the other person grow, but to use the other person to accomplish his own goals. Instead of loving people and using things, the manipulator reverses the value system. He loves things and uses people to help him attain his own goals.

Another substitute for caring is found among people who say they care but act in a way that is inconsistent with their words. After all, it takes a heartless person to say that he does not care for people. Even people who are limited in their caring ability have difficulty saying that they don't care. Caring must be expressed in action. Dr. W. E. Adams, former professor at Southern Baptist Seminary, reminds us of the futility of words without action.

> If words, all kinds of words, consisting of assurances and boasting, of beliefs and creeds, of advice and counsel, of promises and warnings, of pleadings and threats could match the demand of the hour, surely, swiftly, the clouds and fog would lift, chaos and darkness would disappear, tensions and wranglings would be resolved, fear and uncertainty would melt, sin would give place to righteousness, division to unity, conflict to cooperation, war to peace, despair to hope, sorrow to joy, and death to life.[5]

The caring relationship exists when a person communicates through words and actions that he is acting toward the other person in a way that will facilitate the growth of one or both persons.

The Language of Caring

We express to people our caring or lack of caring through the way we communicate. Communication is more than talk; it is the exchange of meaning. Sterling Ellsworth, noted counselor, reminds us that we communicate our meaning through three mediums of communication: our body posture, our voice tone, and the words we speak.[6] The striking factor about our communication is the percentage of our meanings we convey through each of these three mediums. Fifty-five percent is communicated through body posture. Thirty-eight percent is communicated through voice tones. Only 7 percent is communicated through the actual words we speak. Thus, a person communicates with his entire being.

Consider how we communicate with our *body posture.* Body posture involves gestures, facial expressions, the way we walk, the way we sit, and numerous other actions. The gestures we make are some of the most explicit forms of communication. A clenched fist may communicate defiance, aggression, or hostility. A pointed finger often communicates an accusative attitude or a paternal stance in a relationship. Applause is the use of the hands to communicate approval or appreciation. A raised hand may communicate a request for permission or a decision reached in a vote, depending on the setting. Numerous other gestures are made with the hands as a means of communicating.

Facial expressions communicate joy, sadness, depression, fear, and a variety of other emotions. Facial expressions often reflect whether or not a person is finding satisfaction and meaning in life.

The Old Testament provides a classic example of this type of communication.

Moses was up on the mountain with the Lord for forty days. . . . "At that time God wrote out the Covenant—the Ten Commandments—on the stone tablets. Moses didn't realize as he came back down the mountain with the tablets that his face glowed from being in the presence of God. Because of this radiance upon his face, Aaron and the people were afraid to come near him (Ex. 35:28-30, TLB).

Like Moses, we communicate through facial expression and at times are not aware of it. The awareness exists in the persons who receive the communication.

The way we walk can be a means of communication. A hurried walk may communicate anxiety or heightened anticipation. A slow walk may communicate relaxation, or depression, or fatigue.

"It's not what he said, it's the way he said it." Such is a classic illustration of the meaning we communicate through our *voice tone.* The volume, the pitch, and the inflections of the voice combine to communicate meaning.

We have in our home a small puppy. That puppy knows the meaning of very few spoken words. Yet it is possible to communicate with her, not through what we say but through how we say it. When she is scolded, she responds with a body posture that is sorrowful. She tucks her tail between her hind legs and "mopes." When she is spoken to in a kind or cheerful manner, she responds affectionately. If an animal can receive communications through voice tones, why should we doubt that persons, created in the image of God, should not be able to receive such communication in a more effective manner?

On one occasion, when I shared with a group of pastors the amount of communication given through these three mediums, one pastor responded, "It frightens me when I realize that after I have carefully studied and outlined my sermon, I am only 7 percent prepared." In like manner, as I write these words, I am conscious of the fact that I may communicate to you only 7 percent of what I would like to convey. The actual words carry only a small payload of our language of caring.

It would be a mistake to consider the impact of any of these three mediums of communication exclusive of the other two or the setting in which the communication takes place. The three are interrelated, and it is when there is consistency in what all three mediums communicate that the message we send becomes credibile. When there is inconsistency among these mediums of communication, the receiver likely will feel as Isaac must have felt when he was deceived by Jacob and commented, "The voice is the voice of Jacob, but the hand is the hand of Esau" (Gen. 27:22).

The language of caring consists not only in the meanings we *send* to others, but also in the extent that we can *receive* the messages that other people seek to send our way.

Carl Rogers has described the difficulties that people often experience in trying to communicate their meanings to others. He pictures a person trapped in a dungeon, trying to make contact with persons on the outside. Anxiously, the person taps on the wall of the dungeon as he repeatedly asks, "Can anybody hear me? Is anybody there?" Then one day he hears a faint tapping on the other side and knows his message has been received. "Thank God, somebody heard me," is his heartwarming reply.[7]

Receiving the messages that other people try to send involves more than hearing with the ears. It involves listening with sensitivity, using all the channels we have for receiving messages—listening not only to the words, but for the meaning that the person is trying to convey. Just as we send messages through various mediums, we also possess various mediums for receiving messages. The words and voice tones are received through the ears. The body postures are observed by the eyes. These signals are processed through the mind and emotions and the meaning is ascertained. To think that we listen only with our ears is to be like the people of whom Jesus spoke when he said, "Having ears, they hear not."

Characteristics of the Caring Relationship

The caring person is one who personifies love in action. Identifiable characteristics are notable in his life.

A basic characteristic of caring is *empathy*. Empathy is the ability to identify with another person. It means being able to understand the situation of another person by putting oneself in his place. Empathy is rooted in the nature of God. The God of the Bible is not one who sits aloof from the world. The writer of Hebrews described the empathy of Jesus when he wrote, "For we have not an high priest which cannot be touched with the feeling of our infirmities; but was in all points tempted like we are, yet without sin" (Heb. 4:15).

Through empathy we seek to understand the attitude, feelings, and questions of another person, but we do not necessarily possess the same attitudes, feelings, or questions. Through empathy we both understand the other person and maintain a separation that enables us to help the person. Both closeness and distance are important in the caring relationship.

Another characteristic of caring is *openness*. *Openness*

means that one is willing to strip away the facades that cover his personhood and allow other people to see who he really is. It takes courage to be an open person. The open person is vulnerable to attacks upon his personhood. Openness requires that he trust other people not to take advantage of his vulnerability. He must also be prepared for the distinct possibility that someone will betray his trust—and some people will. That is why living in an open manner is a courageous thing to do. However, the person who maintains openness toward other persons will find that in most cases persons will be more open and trusting toward him. Thus, relationships are allowed to move beyond superficial social amenities to a deeper level in which mutual caring is evident.

Honesty is a counterpart of openness. The caring person seeks to be honest in his relationships with other people. Paul's admonition, "speaking the truth in love" is the hallmark of the person who is honest in his relationships with others. The honest person first gets in touch with how he feels in a relationship, then shares his honest feelings at appropriate times.

The caring person is a *tolerant* person. Tolerance means accepting another person as he is, even though many differences exist between them. Tolerance means accepting the beauty in the life of the other person and not demanding that the other person be as you are. Tolerance is like watching a sunset. One reason we can enjoy a sunset is because we cannot force it to change; we can only enjoy it. So it is with people; we should be able to enjoy them as they are, without insisting that they change.

Tolerance does not imply that we do not seek to witness to the other person or influence his behavior. It does imply, however, that we do not force another person to conform to our ideas or beliefs. Authentic witness and influence grows out of a relationship of mutual acceptance, which is tolerance in the best sense.

* * *

"I looked on my right hand, and beheld, but there was no man that would know me: refuge failed me; no man cared for my soul" (Ps. 142:4). One can feel the loneliness that the psalmist must have been experiencing when he wrote these words. To not care or be cared for frustrates our growth as persons. But to care and be cared for optimizes that growth. Is that why Jesus stated, "If ye keep my commandments, ye shall abide in my love; even as I have kept my Father's commandments, and abide in his love. These things have I spoken unto you, that my joy might remain in you, and that your joy might be full. This is my commandment, That ye love one another, as I have loved you" (John 15:10-12)?

Growth Experiences

1. Your Significant Others
   - Make a list of the significant people in your life?
   - How are they contributing to your growth? How are you contributing to their growth?
   - What changes do you need to make in these relationships to achieve more growth for yourself and the other persons?
2. The Meaning of Love
   - Read carefully 1 Corinthians 13 from several translations of the Bible. Then write your own paraphrase of "The Meaning of Love." What changes do you need to make in your behavior to more adequately express love and care to other persons?

3. Cheap Imitations
   - Think of times when someone "faked it" in expressing care for you. How did that make you feel?
   - Think of times when you "faked it" in expressing care for others. How did your faking get in the way of building an authentic relationship with that person?
4. Communicating Care
   - Think of a time when a person communicated beyond any doubt that he really cared for you as a person? How did his caring make you feel? What did he do or say that convinced you that he cared for you in an unselfish way?
   - Seek to become more aware of the ways people communicate caring or lack of caring. But don't try to become a "psychologist" who analyzes and judges other people. That's not caring! Notice people in terms of the following:
     - The distance they place between themselves and other people.
     - The body postures that communicate care or lack of care.
     - The voice tone that communicates joy, sadness, anger, indifference, or fear.
   - Practice really listening to other people. Look, feel, hear, seek to understand. Do this not only with your friends but also with people you do not like. Listen without judging, falsely reassuring, or taking responsibility for the other person. Then evaluate the depth of communication that has occurred between you and other persons because you were willing to listen.

CHAPTER 4

TENDING: To Thine Own Self Be True

Slow me down, Lord!
Ease the pounding of my heart by the quieting of my mind.
Steady my hurried pace with a vision of the eternal reach of time.
Give me, amid the confusion of the day, the calmness of the everlasting hills.
Break the tensions of my nerves and muscles with the soothing music of the singing streams that live in my memory. Help me to know the magical, restoring power of sleep.
Teach me the art of taking minute vacations, of slowing down to look at a flower, to chat with a friend, to pat a dog, to read a few lines from a good book.
Remind me each day of the fable of the hare and the tortoise, that I may know that the race is not always to the swift—that there is more to life than increasing its speed. Let me look upward into the branches of the towering oak and know that it grew great and strong because it grew slowly and well.
Slow me down, Lord, and inspire me to send my roots into the soil of life's enduring values that I may grow toward the stars of my greater destiny.
In Jesus' name, Amen.

—*Author unknown*

I always wondered what it would be like to take part in one of those groups. They were referred to in various ways—sensitivity groups, growth groups, T-groups, and numerous other names. Most of my experience with such groups had been negative. So while I wondered what it would be like, I did not seek out opportunities to take part in one. But I did take part in one. Since then I have participated in and led numerous others. Here is how it all started.

For five years I had attended George Peabody College. I lacked one course completing all the requirements for my doctor's degree. When I looked at the schedule of classes to be offered that semester, the alternatives were few. Then I saw a course titled "group dynamics." The time of the class was compatible with my schedule, so I registered for it.

In the class session, I found myself in a room with twelve other persons, all of whom were about as skeptical of the class as I was. At our first session, we shared reasons why we registered for the class. One student stated, "I think it's important to be aware of what's going on inside you. That's why I registered. I hope the class will help me to get more in touch with myself."

His words have continued to provoke thought. The "thought seed" he planted and my subsequent cultivation of it have led me to several conclusions. First, it is possible for a person to be out of touch with himself. This possibility is validated by the biblical statement, "If we say we have no sin, we deceive ourselves" (1 John 1:8). Second, when a person is out of touch with himself, he robs himself of growth potential. Third, a person can learn to be more in touch with himself. He can learn not to deny or fear what is going on inside him, but face it. Finally, when a person faces his inner feelings and recognizes them for what they are, he can begin to deal with them responsibly.

The Whole Self

We often refer to our minds, emotions, and bodies as though each exists apart from the other two. A more realistic and functional view, however, is to consider that each of these three areas overlaps into the other two. They may be viewed as three interlocking circles. Each circle exists in its own right but each interlocks into the other two. To deny the relationship is to encourage disunity, which prohibits a person from experiencing wholeness in living.

One of the secrets of being "together" as a whole person is to allow mind, body, and emotion to communicate with each other. I use the word "secret" because it is possible for a person to act as though each part of this triad exists separate and apart from the other two. Such, however, is not the case, although many people act as though they are separate.

The human being is rational. Yet his rationality is often

affected by his emotions and physical condition. Each person is a "feeling" person, but his feelings can be affected and altered by his rationality. Each person is a physical being, yet his physical condition can be affected by his emotions and rationality. To neglect any of the three areas is to rob ourselves of growth opportunities.

In taking a holistic approach to our growth as persons, we should not fear facing our emotions. Only as we recognize our emotions are we in a position to begin to exercise necessary controls over them, rather than letting them have full sway over us.

In like manner, we need to learn to listen to our bodies. Our bodies constantly strive to maintain equilibrium. To maintain that equilibrium, the body has a language it seeks to communicate. Its only way of talking is through the feelings it projects upon the mind and emotions. When it is tired, it responds slowly and may ache. When it is rested and well cared for, it provides an adequate home in which our minds and emotions may live. At times the body has a hard time communicating with the rest of the self. If its message goes unheard for a long period of time, the result may be a break down of the body. In other words, the body may become ill. The extent to which we are capable of allowing this triad to function in unison is a factor that relates to our ability to grow as persons.

Every normal person is the victim of attacks by enemies of the realization of his potential. When these enemies become so strong that the person can no longer cope with them, counseling and therapy are necessary. The suggestions that follow deal with the normal problems encountered by healthy people in everyday life. No one is immune from these problems. Moreover, the problems affect the triad of one's being—the mind, body, and emotions. Learning to handle these problems in a more effective manner leads to growth within a person.

Treating Our Tensions

Tension is a knot in the pit of the stomach, a pain in the back, a headache, the inability to relax, a stiff neck, and a dozen other things. But tension also is the ability to perform the necessary functions of life, to engage in recreation, to share life with those we love. The alternatives are not the presence or absence of tension but the presence of tension in adequate amounts or the presence of too much tension, which can become a destructive force.

The place to begin treating our tension is to understand its sources. Tension comes from two main sources. First, there is internal tension that is a carryover from one's past. It is possible for a person to feel tension when there is no present reason for his feeling. Persons who experience this type of tension usually have learned to feel tense in earlier years and continue to do so, even though there is no apparent reason for it. In order to deal with this type of tension, a person needs to examine his past, as I indicated in chapter two. Often, as one examines his past, knowledge from the past may heap insight into the present. The person begins to realize that the cause of his tension is learned responses which are no longer appropriate.

Second, there are pressures in one's external world with which he must learn to cope. These pressures take the forms of financial distress, broken relationships, close deadlines, and dozens of other factors. Such pressures seem greater today than ever before in history. Technology has contributed to our tension by increasing the rate of change that occurs in our lives. As changes occur, old patterns of living and solving problems must give way to novel approaches.

This demand for novelty places stress upon organizations and individuals alike. The demands of change are often synonymous with tension.

The tension in our bodies may be compared to a reservoir of water, such as a lake. There is a "feed in" stream and a "drain off" stream. The secret to handling tension is to maintain the reservoir at the appropriate level. Obviously, control may be exercised at the two areas, where tension feeds in and where it is drained off.

A person can seek to alter his life to reduce tension that feeds into it. However, not all feed-in can be controlled. The ideal is for the person to try not to expose himself to a greater degree of stress and accompanying tension than his reservoir can adequately handle.

Tension may also be reduced by finding appropriate outlets for it. Each person differs not only in the amount of tension he can adequately handle, but also in the types of activities that are appropriate to drain off tension. For example, I have a friend that spends his lunch hour each day working out in a gymnasium. For him, that is an appropriate outlet for tension. For me, it is not. My outlet involves working at a hobby of refinishing furniture. Doing woodwork is an appropriate outlet for me.

Each person needs to find appropriate outlets for his tension. That is why a hobby can be so important. Vacations can serve as tension outlets, provided they are planned in a way that decreases, rather than increases, the tension a person feels.

The dangers of prolonged, excessive tension are many. Not only is it a threat to physical health; it also can affect a person's mental processes, blurring his logical reasoning. Moreover, it is not uncommon for an overly tense person to create for himself an environment that increases the feed-in of tension. For example, a person who is overly tense on the job may begin to alienate himself from his peers and his employer through bursts of temper or other tension "spill overs." Then a "snowballing" effect takes over. The tense person acts upon his environment and the environment responds, creating situations that serve to increase his tension.

The first step in treating tension is to become consciously aware of it. Listen to the body. Feel the tension. Second, consider what action needs to be taken to reduce the feeling of tension. Finally, find an appropriate outlet where excessive tension can be drained off.

Facing Our Fears

Long ago, Job spoke for every man when he stated, "For the thing which I greatly feared is come upon me, and that which I was afraid of is come unto me" (Job 3:25). Deep within us lies the lingering anxiety about the impermanency of health and life. The presence of this anxiety is partially what Kierkegaard called *The Sickness unto Death.* He referred to man's feeling of despair as "an anxious dread of an unknown something, or of something he does not even want to make acquaintance with." [1] This existential fear is the lot of every man. It began when God told Adam, "But of the tree of knowledge of good and evil, thou shalt not eat of it: for the day that thou eatest of it, thou shalt surely die" (Gen. 2:17). "As it is appointed unto men once to die" (Heb. 9:27) is the New Testament writer's way of reminding us of the impermanency of life on earth.

It was to this deep and abiding existential fear that Jesus addressed himself when he gave men the assurance of life after death. Only faith can minister to this type of fear. Moreover, that faith must be a growing faith as the inevitability and reality of death becomes more vivid and conscious, which is the normal process as we grow older.

While there is an existential fear that only faith in Christ can minister to, there are also those fears that are learned. Through life's experiences, we cultivate within ourselves fearful reactions to situations, objects, and events. Some of these fears are helpful, for they teach us caution and contribute to our well-being. Mark Twain has appropriately stated, "The benefits of a cat sitting on a hot stove is that he will not sit on it twice." To possess realistic fear is healthy and rational.

However, many of our fears are neither healthy nor rational. Such fears rob us of reaching toward our potential. The irrationality of such fear is humorously illustrated by J. Winston Pearce in *The Window Sill of Heaven*.

A man walks up to another and says, "Would you give me a match?" No response. He says again, "I say, friend, would you give me a light?" No response, not even the turn of the head. The first man, irritated now, says, "Listen, buddy, I asked you a civil question. If you do not have a light, you could say so. You could at least be respectful."

Then the second man turns his head, looks the first fellow over from head to toe, and says with emphasis, "So, you want me to give you a match? I give you a match and you will say thank you, and I'll say, 'Quite all right'; you will say, 'Nice day,' and I'll say, 'Yes, isn't it?' You will say, 'Who do you think will win the game this afternoon?' and I'll say, 'Not sure; what do you think?' And you'll say, 'By the way, my name is Tom Brown,' and I'll say, 'Glad to know you, Tom; mine's Jim Smith. Why don't we have a cup of coffee together?' You'll say, 'Fine, let's do,' and over the cup of coffee you will invite me to your home and I'll invite you to my home. I have a daughter. You'll meet my daughter. You'll fall in love with her, marry her, and have a houseful of kids. You'll get sick, die, and leave those kids for me to take care of. I don't like kids. No, I'm not going to give you a match." [2]

Fear does not always reside in external events. Rather it may be an inner state of being; a reaction that the person brings to external events. Therefore, the person is not really afraid of the external. He is afraid of his own ability to cope with the external. For example, a person may not fear change; he may fear his ability to deal with the consequences that change may bring. A person may not fear public speaking; he may fear his ability to perform well in a public speaking situation.

In his book, *Walking Toward Your Fear,* H. C. Brown reminds us that "To fear is to be human. The real issue is not what we would do without our fears; the real issue is what we do with them. Second to the real issue is what we can do to get rid of those fears which handicap us. And finally, what can we do for man and God after we secure liberation from our worst fears." [3]

The title for the book, *Walking Toward Your Fear,* provides a clue for beginning to overcome paralyzing fear. The first step is to face fear. To overcome fear takes faith and courage—faith in God to provide sufficient grace and courage to walk toward our fears.

Typical reactions to fear may be described as three stages: fear, flutter, and flight. We become afraid, feel the inward discomforts of the fear, and then seek to escape from the fearful situation. But as long as we flee from our fears they control us; we do not control them.

How can a person begin to overcome his learned fears? First, he must realize that since he learned to fear, he can learn not to fear. One way to overcome fear is through use of the imagination. In a relaxed state, the person imagines increasingly fearful scenes. A person gradually acquires the ability to tolerate the fearful idea or scene of his imagination. This improvement generally transfers to real-life situations. "The rehearsal of fearful scenes is imagination, while in a state of relaxation . . . has proved to be a robust technique for reducing fear."[4]

A lady with whom I counseled expressed fear of taking a college entrance examination. She had been out of school for ten years and was not sure of her ability as a college student. As we talked, I asked her, "What is the worst thing that could happen to you if you take the test?" "I could fail," she replied. "And would you be able to recover from that failure?" I continued. "Of course," she replied. "Well . . . ," I pondered. "Oh, then there really isn't any reason for me to be afraid," she stated. She took the examination and was admitted to college.

Although imagining fear-evoking scenes has numerous practical advantages, there is good evidence to suggest that real-life exposure to fearful situations can be as or more effective if they are carried out in a gradual or systematic manner. Through gradual exposure to fearful situations, persons can become immuned to fear of the situation. With determination and patience, a person can "walk toward his fears."

Dealing with Depression

A leading physician has estimated that more than 90 percent of today's people suffer some form of depression. This depression ranges in intensity and effect from mild, short-lived neurosis to chronic, psychotic depression that requires clinical therapy. Let's agree at the outset that the depression of which I speak are the times of disappointments with accompanying "low mood" that all people experience. Chronic depression, which extends over a long period of time, or recurring depression alleviated only by frequent periods of elation are not normal. Such depression usually needs the attention of a therapist. A person who is aware that he is a victim of chronic depression needs more help than is offered in the following paragraphs. I propose to offer suggestions to persons who experience the "normal" depressions of life.

The external events of depression are varied. However, the key factor in a depressing situation is not the event per se. It is the depressed person's perception of the event. A depression is the result of a person's perception of a loss of something he values—a love object. The loss causes the person to feel angry, and the anger is turned inward rather than directed outward.

The lost love object may take many forms. The loss of a person in death is usually accompanied by a period of depression. Granger Westberg in *Good Grief* describes depression as the third stage of a ten-stage process through which a person moves as he readjusts to loss in a grief situation.[5]

Love objects are not confined to people. It is not uncommon for persons to cherish unrealistic goals that eventually must be faced with reality. The result may be depression as the person realizes that his unrealistic goals, a product of his fantasy, will not be achieved. On numerous occasions I have counseled with persons who were in the process of "coming down," getting in touch with reality again. These persons had cherished unrealistic expectations for themselves or others in relation to them. For example, one person had recently completed a graduate degree at an outstanding university. All through his studies he had cherished the notion that the completion of the degree would bring him the acclaim of many people, a new job, and a significant increase in salary. It was during his "rebound to reality" that we talked. In the process of the conversation he came to realize that for several months he had been "setting himself up" for a letdown.

Radar people, such as those discussed in chapter 2, often are more inclined toward periods of depression. Since they receive the signals for their behavior from other people, they also project upon other people many expectations. When people do not live up to those expectations, the result may be depression.

Fatigue lessens a person's determination thus contributing to a tendency to depression. One of the characteristics of depression is immobility, a feeling of defeat. The depressed person not only does not act; he often feels that he cannot act. The will to act is lessened when a person is tired.

Most people move through periods of depression to states of renewed normality. Such low periods are normal in the face of a perceived loss. In fact, if a person suffers a loss and does not experience at least some measure of depression, he may be deceiving himself. Furthermore, he may be inviting a delayed reaction to the loss. Delayed reactions are often more difficult to deal with because it is harder for the person to identify the causes of his depression.

The first step in dealing with depression is to "own" it. Such a statement may seem absurd. However, the fact is that people often deceive themselves into thinking that they can bear the loss without becoming depressed. People who see depression as a sign of human weakness or a lack of faith in God may deny their depression. But to deny the pain of depression is to encourage lack of treatment.

The second step in dealing with depression is to try to bring into focus the cause of the depression. The causes of depression often are blurred to the person experiencing it. To bring into focus probable causes of the depression often requires a high degree of objectivity—something which the depressed person may not possess. The process of trying to identify causes of depression is an exercise that helps a person gain this objectivity.

The third step in dealing with depression is to talk about it with someone whom you trust. Talking about one's feelings is functional in helping the person to (1) own the feeling, (2) explore alternatives about the causes of depression, and (3) move out of a state of immobility to a state of action. Talking about one's feelings is an activity that helps to unify the three areas of life—the mental, emotional, and physical. When these three areas of life are integrated, the person's will or ability to determine direction becomes stronger.

A classic case study in depression is found in the Old Testament character, Elijah (see 1 Kings 19). Elijah experienced depression. Reading the circumstances surrounding his depression reveals the causes and treatment of his problem.

The cause of Elijah's depression is clear. First, he was a victim of unrealistic expectations. Following the duel with the prophets of Baal on Mount Carmel, Elijah assumed that he had won the support of his opponents, the leaders of the nation.

Second, he was threatened with loss of life.

"And Ahab told Jezebel all that Elijah had done and withal how he had slain the prophets with the sword. Then Jezebel sent a messenger unto Elijah saying, So let the gods do to me, and more also, if I make not thy life as the life of one of them by tomorrow at this time" (vv. 1-2).

Jezebel's message exploded Elijah's illusion of victory. The necessity of returning to reality contributed to his depression.

Third, Elijah was tired. His energy-draining confrontation with the prophets of Baal at Mount Carmel had left him in a state of physical exhaustion.

His depression is clear in his statement, "It is enough;

now, O Lord, take away my life; for I am not better than my fathers" (v. 4).

The cure for Elijah's depression was twofold. First, God provided him with food and rest (see vv. 5-8). Second, God provided him with the occasion to talk about his depression. "And behold, there came a voice unto him, and said, What doest thou here Elijah?" (v. 13). Elijah talked about how he felt.

This process placed Elijah on the road to overcoming his depression. He experienced a renewal of hope. "So he departed . . . and found Elisha . . . and cast his mantle upon him" (v. 19). Elijah's choice of Elisha as his successor was an expression of his hope that the "cause" would live on.

None of us is exempt from either depression or the possibility of it. When confronted with it, we can find our strength again by owning it and seeking to deal with it constructively and forthrightly.

Getting Over Guilt

Guilt can be a creative tension within a person if it serves to lead him to God in prayer for forgiveness. Guilt may be the consequence of sin which is felt by the person who betrays his ethics and values. God, through Christ, has made possible the forgiveness of sin. "If we confess our sin, he is faithful and just to forgive our sin, and to cleanse us from all unrighteousness" (1 John 1:9). "And you, being dead in your sins . . . hath he quickened . . . having forgiven your trespasses" (Col. 2:13). God's grace of forgiveness is one of the most comforting concepts in the New Testament. But it takes faith to accept this grace. We must believe that God has forgiven our sin when we ask for his forgiveness.

Perhaps one of the reasons it is difficult to believe that God actually forgives our sin is because we often have difficulty forgiving ourselves. Recently, in a counseling session, a lady asked, "Will God forgive me of a wrong I committed several years ago? I have asked him to forgive me." I explained that when we ask for God's forgiveness, he grants it. "But when God forgives us, we have to be willing to forgive ourselves." "That's the most difficult part," she replied. To claim the fullness of God's grace of forgiveness requires that a person forgive himself.

There is another kind of guilt a person may feel that is not related to sin or transgression of God's will. It is guilt that results from a conscience that is "wound too tight." "Let your conscience be your guide" is a common cliche; but it is not a very good rule to live by. Conscience does not tell us what is right or wrong; it tells us whether we have acted according to what we believe to be right or wrong. Conscience is not innate; it is learned.

Conscience is the rules that we have internalized into our value system. The person who has no internalized rules has problems in identity as well as behavior. However, the person who is excessively rule-bound tends to be inflexible in his thinking and behavior. He sets high standards for himself and feels guilty when he fails to achieve them.

An accusative conscience is often the result of the teachings of authority figures in one's past. Out of love and wishes for our well-being, parents and other authority figures help us to develop rules to live by. The fear of punishment and the need for love prompt us to keep the rules set by our authority figures. Gradually we either reject these rules or internalize them into our being. The internalized rules become our conscience. When we keep these rules, we reward ourselves with feelings of self-esteem. When we break the rules, we punish ourselves with feelings of guilt.

Although internalized rules help a person in maintaining

his identity, when he is excessively rule-bound he has difficulty accepting his humanity. Too frequently he punishes himself with guilt feelings. Like the prince of Tyrus, of whom Ezekiel wrote, he needs to be reminded "that thou art a man, and not God, though thou set thine heart as the heart of God" (Ezek. 28:2).

God created us as humans. It's OK to be human. To be otherwise is to attempt to be God. A person who experiences the forgiveness of God with its ethical implications and accepts the reality of his humanity has no reason for the chronic existence of morbid guilt.

Plus Factors

Growth consists of more than learning to adequately handle negative emotions. Life is lived in its fullest when we learn to add the "plus" factors. To handle adequately the negative aspects of life helps us to only "break even." It in no sense helps us to achieve the abundant life of which Jesus spoke, for which he came, and which he offers us.

On a flight from Dallas, Texas, to Portland, Oregon, our route took us over the Cascade mountain range. It was late afternoon and the sun was setting. A kaleidoscope of color tinted the western skies. I realized that if I had been down in the valley beneath the mountains, I could not have seen the beauty of that western sunset. It was only because I was above the mountains that I could enjoy the beauty of it. In the same manner, it is only when we are "out of the valley" that we can know the beauty of living. To realize the abundant life, therefore, we must go beyond merely overcoming the negative, we must realize the positive.

One way to add the plus factor to life is to maintain a *positive mental attitude.* I call it "PMA" because it helps me to keep the necessity of it in my consciousness. Inevitably, a person will face those circumstances that have the potential of defeating him. Tragic disappointments, even monotony, can tempt a person to develop a negative attitude. And a negative attitude can place him in the valley, away from the beauty of life. For his own sake, he cannot afford the luxury of a persistent negative attitude.

A positive mental attitude is enhanced as a person feeds the mind with healthy ideas. I have found two ways to do this. First, a disciplined program of reading is helpful. In addition to Bible reading, I have found it helpful to keep a list of books for reading. Some of the books that have been most helpful are contained in the Appendix at the end of this book. I recommend them as a starting place for you as you work at maintaining your PMA.

Second, a positive mental attitude is enhanced by maintaining caring relationships with other people—people who share life with us, affirm us, and challenge us in ways that actualize our potential. We cannot claim the plus factors in life apart from wholesome relationships with other people.

The plus factors in life are enhanced as we learn to practice the art of thanksgiving. Paul wrote, "In every thing give thanks: for this is the will of God in Christ Jesus concerning you" (1 Thess. 5:18). For Paul, this passage was more than good advice to his readers. It was a way of life for him. Although he encountered difficulties, he had learned the art of thanksgiving, which offered him strength in time of difficulty. His word to us is, "As ye have therefore received Christ Jesus the Lord, so walk in him: Rooted and built up in him, and stablished in the faith, as ye have been taught, abounding therein with thanksgiving" (Col. 2:6-7). There are many pressures that pull us toward ingratitude in life. But developing the art of thanksgiving, which is the will of God for us, can help us maintain the proper focus so essential to our continued growth in the face of all kinds of life situations.

Finally, proper care of the body is essential for putting the plus in life. The television commercial, "When you've got your health, you've got just about everything," captures a basic truth. Paul referred to the body as the "earthly tabernacle." It is the dwelling place of our being. The adequacy of that dwelling place depends to a large degree on how well we care for it. Most of us know the requirements for proper care of the body; fewer of us outwardly do it. As a starting point, consider the following.

Secure enough rest. What is "enough" varies with different persons. Personally, I have discovered that I need a full eight hours sleep to function at my best. Moreover, I have also discovered that when I fail to secure enough rest, it interferes with my positive mental attitude. I tend to become negative in my attitude; sometimes even hostile.

Watch the diet. A proper diet involves more than maintaining the correct weight. It also involves proper nutrition. Unless the body is supplied with the nutrition it needs, it does not function to its optimum capacity.

Take adequate exercise. The body was created to be active. Proper exercise is essential to optimum health. It also is a great way to release tension that may build up in the body.

Engage in wholesome recreation. Recreation is not a luxury. It is essential to good health. As the word indicates, it "re-creates" us, helping us to start afresh on those problems we must solve in our daily responsibilities.

* * *

Jess Lair, a teacher at the University of Montana, wrote a best-seller book entitled *I Ain't Much, Baby—But I'm All I've Got.* His confession, "I ain't much," is simply too modest when one examines his life-style as described in the book. However, the second part of the title is true for him as well as all of us. "I'm all I've got," is a universal truth. Therefore, to experience the most growth and joy in life, one must heed the admonition, "To thine own self be true."

Growth Experiences

1. Togetherness

   During the next few days, concentrate on how well you keep your body, your mind, and your emotions together.

   - Listen to the body. Become aware of how it feels. Note the tight muscles, the times when you seem to have more energy or less energy.
   - Concentrate on how you really feel about situations you encounter. "Own" those feelings.
   - Use your mind to decide how you will deal with the feelings in your body and your emotions. Remember—to become aware of them does not mean that you give in to them; it means you are ready to act responsibly toward them.

2. Get in Touch with Tension

   Seek to assess the degree of tension you possess.

   - What are the feed-in factors of your tension?
   - What feed-in factors can be eliminated?
   - What outlets do you use to drain off your tensions?
   - What changes do you need to make to drain off more tension?

3. Face One of Your Fears

   Think of one thing that you fear.

   - Seek to identify why you fear that object or event. Where or how did you learn to fear it? How does that fear get in the way of your growth as a person?

- Close your eyes and imagine yourself confronting and conquering that fear. Imagine the worst thing that could happen to you in this situation. Repeat this exercise several times over the next few days until you are aware that your fear is diminishing.
- Walk toward that fear. In the next few days, place yourself in the actual situation that causes fear. Hang in there. Conquer the fear—don't let it conquer you.

4. Examine Your Depression

   Think of a time when you were depressed.

   - What did you lose or fear losing that caused your depression?
   - What factors contributed to your getting over your depression?
   - What does this event teach you about how to deal with future depressions?

5. Good-bye to Guilt

   Think of a time when you felt guilty even though you had not really done anything wrong.

   - Write a paragraph on what you believe to have been the causes of that guilt.
   - The next time you face a similar situation, remind yourself that its OK to be a human being. Thank God for his love toward you as a human being.

6. Focus on Plus Factors

   - Make a list of the thing that you can honestly thank God for. Carry these with you wherever you go. When negativism makes inroads on your attitude, study the list and express thanks to God for those things.
   - Assess how you are caring for your body. Do you secure enough rest? What about the diet? Are you overweight? Do you get enough exercise? Make some specific plans for better care of your body.

CHAPTER 5

INVESTING: No Deposit—No Return

If you insist on saving your life, you will lose it. Only those who throw away their lives for my sake and for the sake of the Good News will ever know what it means to really live.

—Mark 8:35

Be not deceived; God is not mocked, for whatsoever a man soweth, that shall he also reap.

—Galatians 6:7

There is a law of sowing and reaping that operates in life. A person reaps what he sows. The negative aspect of this law was stated by Paul when he said, "Be not deceived; God is not mocked, for whatsoever a man soweth, that shall he also reap" (Gal. 6:7). In regard to human relations, Jesus stated the positive aspect of the law succinctly, "As you would that men should do to you, do ye also to them likewise" (Luke 6:31). While seeking a positive return from others is not the primary motive for treating other people in a fair and compassionate way, it is nonetheless true that people usually respond toward us in the manner in which we have responded toward them. The Golden Rule is a statement about the law of sowing and reaping.

The law is also true in regard to how we expend our resources in life. When, through our attitudes and actions, we act upon the environment, the environment returns to us rewards or punishments in proportion to and consistent with the investments we have made. It is as though we are shouting into a canyon that returns the echoes of our voices. The volume of the echo is proportionate to and consistent with the voice that shouts. If there are no shouts, there are no echoes. "No deposit—no return" is more than an inscription on a soda bottle; it is a law of life. Hosea reminded Israel of this law when he said, "For they have sown the wind and they shall reap the whirlwind" (Hos. 8:7).

The law can either be a blessing or a curse. The result depends on us. We can shrink back from life and receive little reward or we can invest wisely and courageously in life and reap the rewards of noble effort.

In previous chapters I have stated that we grow as we deepen our self-understanding and awareness and as we relate to people in a caring manner. It is my purpose in this chapter to set forth support for the idea that the way we invest our time, gifts, and energy can be a means of growth for us as persons.

Our Assets

The assets we have to invest are our gifts, time, and energy. These assets are God-given. What we do with them is up to us. We can invest them wisely or squander them. Jesus spoke of the responsibility of wise and courageous investment in life in Matthew 25:14-30. The people who invested their resources wisely received the affirmation of God and joy in life. The person who was afraid to invest was disapproved and lost even that which he had.

The New Testament teaches that we possess spiritual gifts. Paul, in 1 Corinthians 12-14, enumerates several of these spiritual gifts. In Ephesians 4, he discusses the purposes of these gifts. The first of these purposes is "for the perfecting [maturing] of the saints." Thus, the gifts we possess are for the purpose of growing toward maturity and helping other people in their growth pilgrimages.

The Bible describes two kinds of time, *kairos* time and *chronos* time. *Kairos* time is the fullness of time, the expectant moment that blossoms into reality. It was this kind of time to which Jesus referred when he said, "The time is fulfilled, and the kingdom of God is at hand" (Mark 1:15). Paul referred to *kairos* time when he wrote, "But when the fulness of time was come, God sent forth his Son" (Gal. 4:4). To believe in *kairos* time is to have a trust in God and his providence. Part of our stewardship of time is waiting for the *kairos* moment to come.

The other kind of time is *chronos* time. God controls *kairos* time but *chronos* time is left to our control. *Chronos* time is ours to invest. Nothing measures our values so much as the way we invest our time. The values we hold in high esteem are the recipients of our investment of time. Furthermore, the investment of our time brings dividends in proportion to our investments.

Energy consists of three kinds—physical energy, emotional energy, and mental energy. These three types of energy are related and cannot be separated from each other.

Through investing, we convert gifts, time, and energy into other things, such as money, love, and growth.

Our Motives

The investments we make in life always arise from our motivation. We are prompted to act in order to meet felt needs. Furthermore, our needs vary in kind and intensity. Maslow gives us insight into man's basic motivating factors in his "Hierarchy of Needs." The word "hierarchy" is used to indicate that the needs on the lower part of the pyramid, while not being the most important needs in terms of growth, take precedence over the growth needs on the top part of the pyramid.

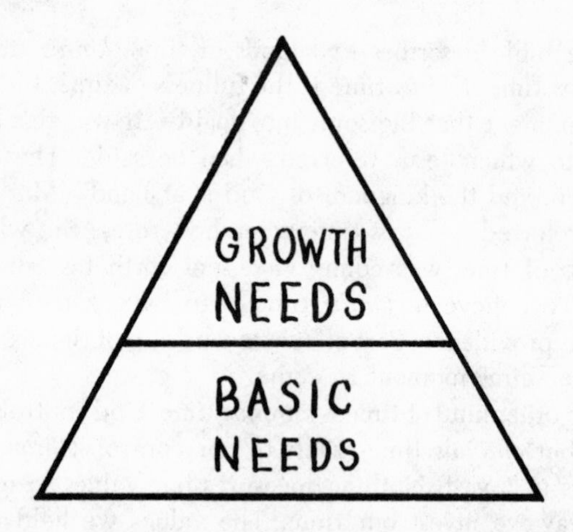

Obviously, we're motivated to meet our basic needs for food, shelter, water, air, and sleep. These needs must be met in order for us to survive. In addition to these needs, we also feel needs for safety and security. Thus, our first concern in existing as persons is to care for those needs that are essential for survival. Once we meet these needs for survival, however, our attention can be directed toward making our survival more secure. Thus, we seek safety and security.

Although the meeting of basic needs is essential to growth as persons, the achievement of these needs does not necessarily assure that we will continue to grow as persons. Once the basic needs are met, a person has to reach out toward the meeting of other needs in order to continue to grow. Such needs are referred to by Maslow as "growth needs."

Growth needs are of three types. First, a person feels a need to love and be loved, to belong to other people and to feel that other people belong to him. In pursuit of love needs, a person may engage in numerous activities. Marriage is one of God's institutions for the meeting of the need for love. "And God said, 'it is not good that man should live alone; I will make a helpmeet for him'" (Gen. 2:18). One of the primary reasons for church involvement is the person's pursuit of stimulation to meet his need to belong to other people and feel that other people belong to him.

A second growth need is the need for self-esteem and the esteem of others. The two esteem needs are inseparable. The esteem of others contributes to self-esteem. Self-esteem prompts a person to act in a way that more likely will elicit the esteem of others. The feeling that one is worthwhile and that other persons consider him worthwhile is a primary factor in growth.

The highest growth needs are needs that help a person "to be that self, which one truly is. . . ." Self-actualization needs prompt a person to seek:

- Wholeness, the feeling that one is integrated as a person.
- Meaning, the pursuit of purpose.
- Aliveness, a feeling of spontaneity and self-regulation
- Self-sufficiency, a feeling of autonomy and independence in which a person does not need other persons in order to be oneself.[1]

The basic needs of man have to be met if he is to survive. The danger is that we may spend more than enough time and energy in the pursuit of basic needs to the neglect of growth needs. When this happens, a person sets limits on his growth. Not having adequate growth goals, the person does not direct his resources toward being a growing person.

Work Investments

Obviously one of the reasons people work is to meet the basic needs of life. The basic needs—food, shelter, safety, and security—are the motivating factors that cause a person to keep a job. But a job can and should be a means of growth.

One Sunday morning in a small town, the tragic news was announced that a leading physician in the community had taken his life. A few weeks later the people of the town learned that this man had been unhappy in his occupation. He never wanted to be a physician. His father who was also a physician had exerted strong influence on him; and he had chosen his vocation to please his father rather than himself. The choice of a vocation should be one where a person finds fulfillment.

Historically, the choosing of a job was often a once-in-a-lifetime decision. Today it is different. A person may choose or have opportunity to choose his work several times during his lifetime. What criteria should be used in choosing an occupation?

Any job with adequate salary can provide for the basic needs of a person provided the person manages well the income from it. If a person does not manage that income well, more income may not solve the problem. More income may be an impetus to a poor management of a larger income.

Let's assume a person has a choice between two jobs, Job A and Job B. Both jobs provide the sufficient income to meet basic needs. What criteria should be used in choosing between the two jobs?

First, consideration should be given to the expression of one's interest and abilities. The New Testament concept of spiritual gifts can find expression not only through the gathered church but also the church scattered at work. Spiritual gifts are those God-given and acquired abilities that are committed to the Holy Spirit's use for the "building up of the body of Christ." Each Christian is a part of that body. The use of spiritual gifts not only should help others; they should also help the person in his own growth. When these gifts are consistent with the activities that are called for in a person's job, there is no conflict within the person between what he wants to do and what his job requires him to do.

Second, consideration should be given to the challenge the job offers. A job that challenges a person encourages his personal growth. History is filled with people who have experienced growth by accepting a job that was a challenge yet within the range of their potential. The challenge helped them to reach part of that potential.

Third, consideration should be given to the opportunity the job offers for Christian witness and ministry. "Give me a place to stand and I can move the world," was the assertion of Archimedes. Does the job offer a person a "place to stand" and witness and minister to others in Christ's name?

A final consideration should be given to the amount of resources required in the job. A job should be a means of expression of one's self, but it should not be the only consuming interest a person has.

Wayne E. Oates, in *Confessions of a Workaholic*, describes a phenomenon that is all-too-prevalent in our culture. Oates writes,

> Workaholism is a word which I have invented. It means addiction to work, the compulsion or unsatiable need to work incessantly. A definition of the workaholic . . . is a person whose need for work has become so excessive that it creates noticeable disturbances or interferes with his bodily health, personal happiness, and interpersonal relationships, and with his smooth social functioning.[2]

If a person's identity exists more in what he does than in who he is, he is a likely victim for workaholism. For the workaholic, the desire to work is insatiable. Even when basic needs are met, he may continue to work harder to acquire more of that which he really does not need. When this happens, a job is not a means of growth; it is a stumbling block to growth, fostered by the person's growth diet being out of balance. If a person invests an inordinate amount of his resources on the job, the returns may be bitter indeed as his relationships with his family and friends begin to feel the strains of neglect.

Family Investments

A family begins with the basic commitment of two people to establish life together. The goal is the establishment of relationships that result in the mutual growth and happiness of each person. The realization of this goal requires much more than the initial investment; it requires continuous attention. A young lady, recently divorced, commented about her problems in married life, "We never built a life together," she said. "When we had leisure time, we spent it with friends. We always existed in relationship to them, never as a married couple in our own right." The establishment of a life together is essential to fulfillment in marriage. Unless that shared life is sought after by both parties, the marriage will not yield the mutually satisfying results that it should.

The relationships of marriage provide unlimited potential for personal growth for each of the marriage partners. Each can help the other to grow in personhood. And it is when each is growing toward that person he wants to be that a marriage offers the greatest happiness. When a couple becomes "growth partners" in which each seeks to actualize not only his own but the other's personal potential, marriage finds its greatest fulfillment.

Parents cannot help but be aware of the physical growth of a child. That growth begins at a rapid rate and slowly declines as the years go by. However, growth in personhood is the opposite. It begins slowly in infancy and progresses at a more rapid pace as a child moves toward adolescence. Conflicts between parents and adolescents are often caused by the adolescents' need to become persons in their own right and the parents' reluctance to allow them to do so. But allow them they must if parents are to act in the best interest of their children. In fact, parents should—and many parents do—become facilitators of the growth of personhood in their children. To facilitate that growth is an unselfish act in which parents are "giving away" a relationship they have cherished. But failure to do so stymies the growth of both parents and the child.

What I am saying is that within the family there exists tremendous potential for growth of persons, providing family members commit themselves to growing and helping other members grow. This basic investment is essential if the family is to reap dividends that are satisfying.

Is this investment being made? Obviously, there are many happy families today. That fact should not be forgotten as we look at the problem areas in family life.

Divorce is all too common; approximately one out of four marriages ends in divorce. The number of parents who are being forced to raise their children without the aid of husband or wife has increased more than ten million since 1970. Ten percent of all children under six in 1970 were living in single-parent families. This means that one child out of six will live in a one-parent family before his eighteenth birthday. This rate is almost double the rate of ten years ago.

Refusal of either parent to accept custody of the children

upon divorce seems to be happening more often today. Parentless and homeless children become the custody of the courts for placement in foster homes. Some of these children feel such sharp hurt and rejection that they have a difficult time recovering from these emotional injuries.

Many unhappy marriages endure until the children leave home to pursue their own life-styles. Then after the children are on their own the marriage dissolves in divorce. In our busy world, parents tend to be spending less time teaching, disciplining, and playing with their children. Parents work outside and away from the home. Therefore, they have less time to spend in activities with their children. In many situations a child spends more time with a passive baby-sitter than with a participating parent. An interview study of middle-class family fathers reported fathers spending an average of fifteen to twenty minutes a day playing with their one-year-old infant. An observational research project revealed that fathers spend 37.7 seconds per day talking with their infant.[3]

Such information leads to the conclusion that we are not investing what we should in family life. A greater investment should be made. The family offers so much growth potential, yet it can be the seedbed of deep pain unless adequate investment is made.

People Investments

Robert was a young man, no more than thirty. He called and asked, "Can I talk to you? I need help." As we talked, he related his story. He had come to Nashville to find a job after losing his job in Charlotte, North Carolina. He had no friends in Nashville, he was broke, and he wanted to go home. I found him a place to stay for the night and told him I would get him a bus ticket to Charlotte if he would come back the next morning. But he did not return. Was he honest with me? Or was he trying to "con" me into giving him money? I really don't know. But in either case, he was a young man who needed help. He had never found a purpose in life. His life had no significant meaning. He needed someone who was willing to invest himself in trying to redeem his life.

Jack was a student at Belmont College. In the psychology class I taught, students who wished to do so were allowed to take a personality inventory test. Jack's test indicated that he was tense. In fact, on a scale from one to ten he rated as high in tension as a person could be. After I interpreted the test to the class, Jack lingered after class to talk to me. "I need to talk to you," he said, "because I'm all knotty inside." Then Jack shared with me the ordeal he had gone through. He had surgery on his knee and the doctors discovered a malignant tumor behind his kneecap. He had not told his parents because he was afraid they would "baby" him. And he didn't want pity. He wanted to "be a man." But being a man was extremely difficult for him since his surgery. He needed someone to listen, to understand, yet not take the responsibility for his being.

Wally was only six years old when the accident occurred. His family was vacationing in Texas when a car careened on a telephone booth where his mother was making a call. His mother was killed, leaving Wally's father with the task of rearing Wally and his nine-year-old sister. As a family, we began a "ministry" to Wally. My wife, realizing that Wally no longer had the benefit of well-prepared meals, often invited Wally to spend the night at our house with our son, Mark. On those nights, she made dinner a bit special, preparing home-cooked dishes like Wally's mother might have prepared. Providing Wally with those meals was a joy for all of us. Wally enjoyed the food; we received satisfaction from investing ourselves to help Wally. We grew in our Christian compassion because we invested ourselves in Wally.

Paul wrote, "For we know that the whole creation groaneth and travaileth in pain together until now" (Rom. 8:22). Regardless of whatever else Paul meant, I think he was trying to tell us that everybody hurts a little and some people hurt a lot. The pains of other people provide us with occasions to minister to them and opportunities to grow as Christian persons.

W. O. Thomason, in *The Life Givers*, describes how our willingness to invest ourselves in the lives of other people results not only in helping them, but in helping us also.

> There are words that describe how a life giver feels because of his work. He thrills. He hopes. He lives. In giving insight he gets excitement. In giving hope he gets hope. In giving life he gains his life. Herein is the essence of the saying, "He who will lose his life shall save it." The tide of evil moves relentlessly upon all people. Surely we shall all perish unless some of us act courageously to stem this tide.[4]

Finding opportunities to help people, to invest ourselves in redeeming their lives, is not difficult. Such people are all around us. We need only to become sensitive to the hurts they are trying to share. Browning wrote:

> Earth's crammed with heaven,
> And every common bush afire with God;
> But only he who sees, takes off his shoes,
> The rest sit round it and pluck blackberries . . .

God often comes to us in the form of a need expressed by other people. When we learn to be sensitive to those needs, we help other people and achieve growth for ourselves.

* * *

Several years ago, my wife and I opened a small bank account in our son's name. He was proud of it and immediately set a goal of reaching one thousand dollars in the amount of his account. Each time he would save a few dollars, we would take it to the bank and deposit it. It seemed that he would never reach his goal. But one day when we got our bank statements through the mail, he was delighted to learn that his goal had been achieved. My son thought he had about nine hundred dollars in his account. He had failed to consider that he was drawing interest on his money. Because he had invested his money, it grew. That's the way our investments in life work for us.

Growth Experiences

1. Analyzing My Assets
   - Read 1 Corinthians 12-14. Make a list of the gifts you believe you possess. Discuss your list with other persons to discover if they have observed those gifts in you.
   - Conduct a time and motion study for one week. Keep a record of how you spend each hour of your time and the types of activities you do. What does this study teach you about how you are using your assets?
2. My Motives
   - What activities do you engage in to meet your basic needs?
   - What activities do you engage in to meet your growth needs?
   - What additional activities do you need to begin to en-

hance your growth as a person?

- What activities do you need to eliminate to enhance your growth as a person?

3. Daily Work
   - Does your occupation provide you with opportunities for personal growth? If so, in what ways? How can you better maximize growth opportunities in your occupation?
   - In what ways does your job offer opportunities for Christian witness and ministry? To what extent are you taking advantage of these opportunities?
4. The Family
   - In what ways do members of your family encourage your personal growth?
   - In what ways do you encourage the personal growth of other members of your family?
5. Leisure Time
   - What opportunities for personal growth are offered through your church and community?
   - To what extent are you taking advantage of these opportunities?

CHAPTER 6

WORSHIPING: God Is Able . . .

You must learn to know God better and discover what he wants you to do.
—*2 Peter 1:5*

A recent survey by a leading magazine indicated that belief in the existence of God is still widely spread in our culture. "People still seek answers to the great religious questions that human beings have addressed themselves to for centuries, and still ache to believe that someone is minding the store, that there is something beyond our personhood and collective reach." [1] For most people, the belief in the existence of God is no major question. The major question is "How does he exist?" Or, "What is the nature of his existence?" Furthermore, they desire to know how a person comes to know God in a dynamic way so that he can become a powerful force in one's life.

The growing person must have a growing concept of God. Childlike faith is essential to our entrance into the kingdom of God. However, childlike faith does not imply childish faith. God is infinitely greater than we can imagine. If our faith in him is to be adequate to meet the demands of a growing life, we must grow in our perception of his greatness and the power that he can bring into our lives. The poet illustrates this point in a striking manner.

A boy was born mid little things,
Between a little world and sky
He dreamed not of the cosmic rings
Round which the circling planets fly.

He lived in little worlds of thought,
Where little ventures grow and plod
And paced and plowed his little plot,
And prayed unto his little God.

But as the mighty system grew,
His faith grew faint with many scars;
The cosmos widened in his view,
But God was lost among the stars.

Another boy in lowly days,
As he to little things was born,
Yet gathered lore from woodland ways,
And from the glory of the morn.

As wider skies broke on his view,
God greatened in his growing mind;
Each year he dreamed his God anew,
And left the older God behind.

He saw the boundless scheme dilate,
In stars in blossoms sky and clod;
And as the universe grew great,
He dreamed for it a greater God.

As we grow, we must "dream God anew" if he is to have his greatest impact in our lives.

God Is a Person

Because of God's magnitude, people for centuries have felt the challenge to understand God in a rationalistic way. People want to know about God and often engage in intellectual, rationalistic endeavor to understand him. Such endeavors were epitomized by the Greek philosophers. Plato thought of God as a preexistent mind that could be partially understood by becoming aware of the great ideas that existed in the universe. Aristotle conceived of God as the "uncaused cause behind the world."

Such rationalistic endeavor may lead us to affirm the existence of God, but they do not *prove* his existence. Neither do they tell us about what kind of God is "minding the store."

While rationality leads us to understand the existence of God, it takes experience to understand the reality and nature of God. God is a person and that person was revealed to mankind through Jesus Christ. Jesus stated, "He that hath seen me hath seen the Father" (John 14:9). Paul stated, "For it pleased the Father that in him should all fullness dwell" (Col. 1:19). The writer of Hebrews affirmed, "God, who at sundry times and in divers manners spake in times past unto the fathers by the prophets, hath in these last days spoken unto us by his Son" (Heb. 1:1).

Jesus Christ was God who became man. Jesus took God out of the abstract and made him concrete, within our ability to comprehend him. God, through Jesus Christ, became a God we could experience. His concreteness was demonstrated by John who wrote, "That which . . . we have heard, which we have seen with our eyes, which we have looked upon, and our hands have handled . . . declare we unto you" (1 John 1:1-3).

Through the coming of Jesus, God made it possible for us to know him fully. How do we come to know him? Not merely by learning about Jesus Christ, but by following him, by committing ourselves to his way of life, by experiencing him in our lives. The person who commits himself to follow

Jesus begins to experience in his life the reality of God. His experience confirms his commitment. He knows God because God is a vital, living, powerful force in his life.

God is not merely a doctrine to be believed; he is a person to be experienced. As we experience him in our lives, our doctrine of him begins to develop. Without faith in Jesus Christ, God remains an abstraction that we cannot fully grasp. But through faith in Jesus Christ, God is experienced as a living person in our lives.

God Is Within Us

In John Masefield's drama, *The Trial of Jesus*, the Roman centurion who commanded the troops that crucified Jesus reports to Pilate after he performs the task. Pilate's wife, Procula, begs the centurion to tell her the story. She asks, "Do you think he is dead?" "No, Lady," the centurion replies, "I don't." "Then where is he?" she inquires. He responds, "Let loose in the world, lady, where neither Roman nor Jew can stop his truth." The resurrection of Jesus resulted in his being "let loose in the world." Moreover, the place where he resides in the world is in the lives of persons who commit themselves to follow him. Jesus stated that after his resurrection and ascension, his followers would receive power—the power of the Holy Spirit.

The Christian has within him the same power that raised Jesus Christ from the grave. "And God hath both raised up the Lord, and will also raise us up in his own power" (1 Cor. 6:14). When a person commits his life to Jesus Christ, he receives that resurrection power in his life. The Holy Spirit takes up residence in his being.

The indwelling of God in our lives in the presence of the Holy Spirit was emphasized by Paul when he wrote, "Ye were sealed with the Holy Spirit of promise, which is an earnest of our inheritance" (Eph. 1:13-14).

In San Ildefonso Indian pueblo near Santa Fe, New Mexico, there lives an aged Indian woman named Maria Poveka. Maria is internationally famous for the black pottery that she has made. She discovered how to make that pottery by accident. One day, after treating the pottery for baking, she placed it in the oven and left it either too long or at a temperature that was too intense. When she took it from the oven, it was beautiful and glossy and jet black. At first, she was ashamed of her mistake. She hid the pottery from the retailer who came frequently to purchase the pottery for sale in a gift shop in Santa Fe. However, with hesitation she showed him the pottery, thinking he probably would not be interested in it. The retailer recognized the pottery as a "thing of beauty." He encouraged her to make more just like it. Thus, she began a distinct art, making black pottery, which brought her international fame. Soon other Indians began to make black pottery, and many of them succeeded. To maintain her identity as the originator of black pottery, Maria was forced to sign each piece of the pottery she made. Thus, the signature "Maria Poveka" on the bottom of the work of art told people that the pottery belonged to Maria—and no one else. The Holy Spirit is "God's signature" that we belong to him; that he lives within us to give us the power to grow.

Paul's use of the word "earnest" in relation to the Holy Spirit (see Eph. 1:14) means the same thing that we mean today when we speak of earnest money being given in a real estate transaction. The earnest money is the purchaser's act of sincerity in which he indicates that he is willing to complete the transaction he has begun. The Holy Spirit within us is God's evidence that "He which hath begun a good work in you will perform it" (Phil. 1:6).

The Fruit of the Spirit

The Holy Spirit is a dynamic power in the life of the believer. Moreover, because of his presence and potential power, he is often subject to misunderstanding and misinterpretation. Two major ideas need to be kept in mind as we allow the Holy Spirit to work in us.

First, the Holy Spirit never calls attention to himself; he calls attention to God through Jesus Christ. When a person experiences redemption, it is because the Holy Spirit has led that person to realize his need for Christ. In the same way, the Holy Spirit continues to point a person to Christ as the person to follow in his daily living and growth.

Second, the Holy Spirit working in the life of the believer produces a deep sense of satisfaction within the person's life. Paul, referring to this deep satisfaction, wrote about the fruit of the spirit. "But the fruit of the spirit is love, joy, peace, long suffering, gentleness, goodness, faith, meekness, temperance" (Gal. 5:22-23). These are the qualities of life that God wants us to possess. They are qualities of life that God is working within us to achieve. Look further at the meaning of the words.

Love is the *agape* referred to in chapter 4. It is the unselfish love God demonstrated in sending Jesus into human history. It is spontaneous. It is given not because someone deserves it, but because the giver has received it from God. Its finest description is in 1 Corinthians 13; its finest embodiment is in Jesus Christ.

C. S. Lewis in his autobiography, *Surprised by Joy,* writes: "Joy is never in our power and pleasure is. I doubt whether anyone who has tasted joy would ever, if both were in his power, exchange it for all the pleasure in the world." The word "joy," is not often used today. However, it was used frequently by biblical writers. John records these words of Jesus, "These things have I spoken with you, that my joy might remain in you, and that your joy might be full" (John 15:11). One of the purposes of Jesus' ministry was to give us joy. Joy is a by-product of one's commitment to Jesus Christ. Joy is freedom—freedom from guilt, freedom from fear, freedom to love, freedom to be, freedom to give, freedom to learn. Joy is the gift of God to a person who allows the Holy Spirit to work in his life.

To the Christians in Rome, Paul wrote, "Now the God of hope fill you with all joy and peace in believing, that ye may abound in hope, through the power of the Holy Spirit" (Rom. 15:13). Note two things: (1) It is God that fills us with peace, and (2) It is through the power of the Holy Spirit that we experience it. *Peace* is lack of inner turmoil. *Peace* is being able to accept oneself. Peace is that feeling deep within that everything is OK. Peace is so basic to Christian experience that it regularly appears with "grace" in Paul's writings. Paul seems to suggest that experiencing the grace of God and a deep sense of peace are inseparable.

Long suffering means patience. Patience is the alternate to frustration and anger. The Holy Spirit working in our lives can help us to develop a more patient approach to frustrating and seemingly intolerable situations.

The two qualities, *gentleness* and *meekness*, of life are so similar that it is difficult to deal with them separately. They refer to a presence of quiet strength in one's life. The meaning of "meekness" refers to a wild animal becoming tame. The strength is still there; it is merely brought under control, not destroyed. Meekness comes as we allow the Holy Spirit to tame our aggressive natures. Meekness is strength under control. The strength is exercised when necessary, but it is exercised judiciously because it is under control and not out of control. Meekness was a quality in the life of Jesus. William Barclay observes, "Only a man who was meek could have both cleansed the temple of hucksters who traded in it and forgiven the woman taken in adultery whom all the orthodoxed condemned."

Goodness does not refer to "goody-goodness." Rather, it refers to generosity. The Holy Spirit leads us to an acute awareness of the generosity of God toward us and the necessity of our being generous in our relationships with other people.

Faith refers to trustworthiness or fidelity. One of the fruits of the Spirit is to become a person on whom others can depend. The person who is faithful is the person who possesses the deep sense of integrity and obligation toward his commitments.

Temperance is self-control. It means taking hold of one's life through the power of the Holy Spirit, seizing the "existential moments" referred to in chapter 2, and becoming a responsible, choosing person. Self-control is inner strength by which a person takes hold of himself, refusing to be swept along by errant desires or impulses. The Holy Spirit is working within us, bidding us to possess these qualities of life. Thus, God is always challenging us to grow—to go on "from here to maturity."

Walking in the Spirit

How do we come to possess these qualities of life? At once we must recognize that possessing the fruit of the Spirit is a lifelong process that requires diligent and enduring effort. A person can advance or regress in the extent to which these qualities are noticeably characteristic of his life.

In reality a person cannot produce this fruit. The fruit is produced by the Holy Spirit as a person cultivates and nourishes his life. When we discipline ourselves to engage in cultivation and nourishment endeavors, the Holy Spirit can work in our lives to provide the fruit.

A primary *cultivation* discipline is prayer. One of the greatest hindrances to our growth as Christians is lack of prayer. When the disciples asked, "Lord, teach us to pray" (Luke 11:1), they were asking Jesus to teach them the discipline of prayer. They had observed this discipline in Jesus and were aware of the power it brought to his life. They wanted that power in their own lives.

"Men ought to pray and not . . . faint" (Luke 18:1). Jesus taught that prayer is the alternative to despair. The person who engages in diligent and persistent prayer discovers power that helps him not to despair when the problems of life rush in upon him. Prayer is the recognition and expression of faith in a powerful God who cares about us and is able to help us overcome disparaging problems in life.

One of the characteristics of prayer should be *reverence for God.* When we pray, we recognize that while "God is for us," he is also other than us. Prayer is coming into the presence of the heavenly Father whose "thoughts are not your thoughts" (Isa. 55:8). Such prayer involves a commitment to do the will of God as God reveals it to us.

Another characteristic of prayer is *sincerity* or *honesty.* God knows our thoughts even before we pray. Therefore, we should have no hesitation in expressing our honest and real requests or feelings. "But when ye pray, use not vain repetitions" (Matt. 6:7). Don't get in a rut with your praying. Learn to pray sincerely and honestly, expressing how you really feel. When you are happy, express that happiness to God and thank him for it. When you are "down," do not hesitate to express those feelings also. Many times when we try to express our real and honest feelings to God in prayer, we get in touch with those feelings in a way that we have not previously experienced. Just getting in touch with them sometimes can be part of the answer to prayer.

Honesty in prayer comes with practice. We must get in touch with how we really feel and express that feeling to God.

A third characteristic of prayer is *spontaneity*. Jesus taught that when we pray we should "enter into thy closet" (Matt. 6:6). It was his way of saying that prayer should not be demonstrative, like the prayers of the Pharisees, but should be personal, between the person and God. In our hurried pace of life, we must learn to "create a closet" in which to pray. What I mean is that we must learn to pray spontaneously wherever we are when we see people or situations about which we should pray. We face a difficult moment, and we pray for God's guidance. We see a "thing of beauty," and we thank God for it. We see a person in deep distress, and we ask for God's grace to abound in his life. I believe that is what Paul meant when he wrote, "Pray without ceasing" (1 Thess. 5:17). When we learn to pray in this manner, we live our lives in the consciousness of God's presence and invite the Spirit of God to help us to become more mature.

A final characteristic of prayer involves being *specific* in the things we pray for. Make your prayers more than vague generalities. Pray for specific things. Write them down. Keep a record of answered prayer. As you record prayer answers, you will receive encouragement to continue your quest in prayer.

Prayer is a *cultivation* discipline. *Personal Bible study* is a *nourishment* discipline. To grow we must feed our spirits on the word of God.

Several plans for personal Bible study are available from

denominational publishing houses. You may wish to explore these plans or devise your own. I find that the plan most helpful to me is the study of books of the Bible. I discovered the joy of this approach several years ago as I spent several weeks "digging in" on the book of Romans. Since then I have sought to move through all the books of the New Testament. I'm still working on some of them. And I still have the Old Testament to go.

Bible study feeds the mind and spirit. It helps us discover the nature and will of God. It keeps primary values in focus. No growing Christian can be without it.

In addition to our personal cultivation and nourishment, we must *share life in the fellowship of the church* in order to achieve maximum growth. Howard Clinebell has stated, "There are many things a person can do alone, but being a Christian is not one of them." Whatever else the New Testament church was, it was first and foremost a fellowship of persons committed to growing in "the way" of Jesus Christ. They affirmed and challenged each other to grow.

Clarence is in his mid-fifties. He is chairman of deacons at a church where I served as interim pastor. "My church opened a whole new dimension of life to me," he said. "Twenty years ago the doctor told me that I had a kidney disease and had no more than two years to live. I don't know why God allowed me to live," he said. "But I didn't begin to really live until about ten years ago when a small group of other people joined with me in starting this church. This church has helped me to grow in my Christian life. I've shared my life with others, and they have shared their lives with me. And that has made life worth living." To share life in the fellowship of the church of Jesus Christ is to join with others in the pilgrimage of Christian growth.

* * *

Take God out of the abstract and find him in the person

of Jesus Christ. Follow that God. Learn about him through the study of his revelation of himself in the Bible. Meet him each day in prayer. Share your experiences with others who experience him in the fellowship of the church. Cultivate and nourish your life and God will help you to grow, according to his will and to your benefit.

Growth Experiences

1. Your Grown-up God
   - Write five words that describe some of the ways that you thought about God when you were a child.
   - At what point in your life did God become more than just a word to you?
   - Write five words that describe some of the ways that you think of God now. Compare these words with your "childhood" words. How are they different?
2. God in Jesus Christ
   - What teachings or activities of Jesus make you feel that God really loves and cares for you?
   - Locate those events or teachings in the New Testament and read them from several translations of the Bible.
3. The Fruit of the Spirit
   - Read Galatians 5:22-23. Write a definition of each fruit of the Spirit in terms of how it should affect changes in your behavior.
4. Walking in the Spirit
   - Begin to practice honesty in prayer. Get in touch with how you feel at this moment and express it to God in everyday language.
   - As you carry out daily routines during the next week, practice spontaneous prayer. Pray for God's power in your life and the lives of others.

- Construct a specific prayer list. Spend some time each day praying specifically for each person or item on the list. Keep a record of the times that prayers are answered. Share your prayer experiences with a loved one or friend.

CHAPTER 7

CHARTING: This One Thing I Do

The striving to find a meaning in one's life is the primary motivational force in man.

—Victor Frankl

Forgetting what lies behind and straining forward to what lies ahead, I press on toward the goal for the prize of the upward call of God in Christ Jesus. Let those who are mature be thus minded.

—Philippians 3:13-15, RSV

Thoughts are but dreams till their effects be tried.

—Shakespeare

"He's only a little boat looking for a harbor." Such was the description of Willie Loman in Arthur Miller's *Death of a Salesman.* And such is the description of many people today. It is because Willie Loman personifies countless other people that Miller's play was so well received. It reminded us that many people have lost their compass in life.

Too often, because of lack of purpose, a large degree of the joy of living is lost. Like scattered ships on the sea that have lost both compass and rudder, people are merely drifting through life with no special direction in mind.

Jesus challenged his followers to a life of purpose and meaning. Such purpose and meaning was discovered by Paul and expressed in his letter to the Philippians. "Forgetting what lies behind and straining forward to what lies ahead, I press on toward the goal for the prize of the upward call of God in Christ Jesus. Let those of us who are mature be thus minded" (3:13-15, RSV).

Since the advent of psychology as a separate discipline

in the late nineteenth century, attention has been given to the effect of purpose and meaning on a person's behavior. While various schools of psychology often disagree on several aspects of human behavior, they are agreed on the importance of purpose as an energizing force in life.

Why is so much attention given to purpose? Because it is purpose that integrates the person, thus enabling him to find meaning in life. Purpose has unifying power. For example, a young man attends college for two years. He is ambivalent about what he wants to do with his life. Then one day he recognizes that he wants to be a physician. He finds a purpose, and his resources—gifts, time, and energy—are directed toward the achievement of that purpose. Thus it is with each of us. Clarity of purpose mobilizes our resources in the pursuit of that purpose. Purpose unifies our efforts and provides energy for achievement, energy that is always present but seldom put to the most productive use unless it is directed toward a goal.

Purpose is found as a person finds goals for his life. Purposeful living is living that is filled with meaning. Milton Mayeroff in his book, *On Caring*, reminds us, "No one else can give me the meaning of my life; it is something I alone can make. The meaning is not something predetermined which simply unfolds; I help both to create it and discover it, and this is a continuing process, not a once and for all." [1]

In this chapter I want to challenge and direct you to clarify some goals for your personal growth. I will not attempt to describe what your goals should be. No one else can do that but you. Your goals must be your decision. My purpose is to provide the criteria for your consideration as you clarify your goals. At the end of the chapter, you will have an opportunity to "have a go at it" in clarifying some of your goals.

Goals Should Be Liberating

If goals give purpose and meaning to life, they must be liberating. While duty is involved in our commitment to goals, it is the lure of these goals that sustains our effort to achieve them. When there is no lure in a goal, the goal becomes a duty rather than a joy. In contrast, when there is a lure in a goal, the goal becomes liberating, freeing us to focus our energy in the pursuit of it.

Duty with its accompanying "ought" and "must" can serve useful purposes, but when it is a pitchfork in a person's back, it diminishes the lure that a person may feel.

There is a sense of divine necessity that the Christian should feel about the purpose of his life, the responsibility that he has to Christ to bid him to "follow me," and the ethical demands of living in a secular culture. However, if all of life is duty, vitality and spontaneity takes a back seat. The stern voice of duty puts shackles on our ankles. Joy is put in cold storage. Freedom is bound with cords of "oughtness." The "fun of life" is taken out of living.

Psychologist William H. Mikesell reminds us:

> When one follows the stern voice of duty with its rod of compulsion, it becomes impossible to possess purpose with its attractive endeavor, its thrill, its appeal that persuades instead of drives. An austere man is not a happy man; austerity takes the zest out of life; purpose puts it back in; austerity turns a man into one that compels himself. Conscience becomes a big policeman and all it does is watch and punish. Duty, in this sense of the term, and purpose are as incompatible as day and night. The duty-bound person may accomplish a great deal, but he could accomplish a great deal more by replacing duty with purpose.[2]

The austere person has difficulty following Jesus' admonition to love one's neighbor as himself. How can he love others and their actions if he finds no joy and purpose in his own?

Goals that are liberating must be arrived at not through rationality alone but through rationality and intuition. After we have expressed the goal, regardless of how lofty it sounds, we must "feel it." As Pascal reminds us, "The heart has reason that reason does not know." A classic example of feeling the lure of a goal was expressed to me by a lady who commented, "When I think of doing what I have decided to do, I feel my heart begin to beat faster."

Christian growth should be a matter of freedom and joy. Unless a goal has lure, it will not be lasting.

Goals Should Be Person Oriented

Many of our resources are directed toward the achievement of goals external to the self. In the process, goals related to growth of the self are often neglected or given minimal attention.

Growth goals may be task oriented. But a task-oriented goal may not be a growth goal. A person may devote so many of his resources to the achievement of a task that he neglects his own need to grow. In pursuit of a task goal, one may abuse the body, dull the emotions, and drain the mind of its potential for creativity. For example, a person may devote his resources to the acquisition of wealth. The wealth does not contribute to his growth as a person. In fact, it may be symptomatic of his lack of growth, toil to seek a feeling of worthwhileness which does not come.

The unifying factor of growth goals is the well-being of the person. Tasks may be performed. Relationships may be established and strengthened. But the primary reason for this activity is the growth of the person.

Goals Should Be Related to Potential

Browning stated, "A man's reach should exceed his grasp, or what's a heaven for." Browning spoke of the necessity of setting goals related to our potential.

While growth goals are personal, the expression of our desires, they always exist outside of us. We project them as a state of being that is beyond or ahead of us. It is almost a universal characteristic that when people talk about their cherished goals, there is a "far-away" look in their eyes indicative of their hopes for something beyond or ahead of them.

Yet, the envisioning of lofty goals is frought with fear. Maslow stated that, "We fear our highest possibilities. We are generally afraid to become that which we can glimpse in our most perfect moments, under the most perfect conditions, under the conditions of greatest courage. We enjoy and even thrill to the Godlike possibilities that we see in ourselves in such peak moments. And yet we simultaneously shiver with weakness, awe, and fear before these very same possibilities." [3]

Perhaps the reason for this fear is the possibility of failure. Rather than to aspire toward that potential and risk failure, we suppress the desire to achieve. The result is that we rob ourselves of potential for growth. Maslow refers to this tendency as the Jonah complex, the fear of facing the destiny that is ours.

I indicated in chapter 4 that failure to achieve unrealistic goals often leads to depression. If a person fails to achieve a goal and experiences the resulting depression, he may decide never to try again. It is time, then, for him to decide what goals are realistic and what goals are beyond his reach. Also, he must be willing to take the risk of failure.

Several factors may be considered in seeking to determine realistic goals for one's life.

First, a person should examine the depth of his commitment to the goals. The extent to which he is committed to a goal influences the amount of time and energy he can allow to "flow freely" into his efforts to achieve the goal. That is why the "reasons of the heart" must be considered in determining goals.

Second, a person must consider the amount of time it will take to achieve a goal. Some goals take a lifetime. Some goals are never fully realized. Goals must be determined in keeping with the amount of time that we have left in our life scripts.

Goals must be made with the time as a major factor for consideration. Obviously, if we knew the exact amount of time we had left in life, we would be able to set our goals more precisely. But we do not know the exact amount of time. We do, however, have a general idea of the amount of time. We have some "norms." The goals of youth, middle adults, and senior adults are influenced in different ways by the time factor.

Goals Should Be Specific

All of us have implicit goals. Usually, they are broad and vague. We "see through a glass darkly" when we consider them. Seeking to reach vague goals is like shooting at a target that is blurred to our vision. We may hit the target, but the probabilities are on the side of missing it.

In *The Strangest Secret,* Earl Nightingale reminds us that the greatest difficulty is not the achievement of goals, but the determination of specific goals. Once we have set a worthy goal, we likely will achieve it. The strangest secret, according to Nightingale, is this: *a person becomes that which he thinks about most of the time.*

If our goals are vague, our concentration upon them will be impaired. If they are specific, we possess clarity of purpose. Here is a good criterion for measuring how specifically a goal is clarified: Is it clear enough to be written down? Francis Bacon stated that writing makes an exact man. Writing down our goals forces us to see them clearly. Furthermore, the process of writing them helps lock them into our consciousness. On frequent occasions my wife asks me to stop by the grocery for a few items as I leave my office at the end of the day on my way home. I learned a long time ago not to trust my memory if the number of items exceeds three or four. I write them down. However, when I get to the grocery, I usually do not need the list. The process of writing down the items I am to buy has stamped clearly into my mind what they are. The same thing happens when we write down our goals. They become a part of us.

Goals Should Be Flexible

On one occasion after leading a Personal Growth Workshop, I asked the participants to bring to the last session an object that symbolized what the experience had meant to them. A man brought two bottles. One of them was empty; the other was partially filled. "The empty bottle symbolizes how my life used to be," he said. "It was hard on the outside, but empty on the inside. The other bottle symbolizes my life now. While it is not completely filled, it is fuller than it was. Furthermore, the bottle is open at the top. There is no lid on it. That means that I am still open to God's revelation and that I continue my quest for fulfillment."

Goals should be precise, but in a sense there's always a tentative quality about them. One of my teachers used to say, "I reserve the right to be smarter tomorrow than I am today. Therefore, I may change my mind."

Since Christian growth is a process that is never completed, the goals we set should never indicate that we plan to reach a specific plateau and stop there. The kingdom of God is within us. The Holy Spirit knows no boundary. God's revelation continues to come to us through life. Therefore, openness to new experiences, new revelations, new goals is consistent with the New Testament teaching "It does not yet appear what we shall be" (1 John 3:2).

Goals Should Be Shared

Once goals have been determined, they should be shared with a group of friends who can give us support for the achievement of those goals. Also, once those goals are shared with someone else, there is a sense in which we deepen our commitment to them through the sharing of them. They may be shared with members of a group at church, family members, or people with whom we work. They may be shared with a group of friends in the community. In any event, once goals have been determined, they should be shared with other people so that other people can serve as a support system to our achievement of those goals.

Your goals are very much like a road map. They tell you which way to go when you come to the crossroads. Which way you go may not matter if you are just driving around for sightseeing. But if you are going somewhere, you need to have the destination in mind and the probable routes that will get you there. Goals should be related to God's will.

Growth Experiences

1. Write Your Goals

Let's begin to work on some goals for your growth in

Christian personhood. Remember, they must be your goals, things that you really want to do or be.

- In terms of self-understanding, I would like to ______
______
- In terms of my relationship to other persons, I would like to ______
______
- In terms of my emotions, I would like to ______
______
- In terms of my mental or intellectual abilities, I would like to ______
______
- In terms of how I use my gifts, time, and energy, I would like to ______
- In my relationship to God, I would like to ______
______

2. Plan Your Actions
   - List at least one activity you plan to begin within the next thirty days to reach each of the above goals.
3. Share It
   - Share with at least one other person the goals you have set.
4. Check Up

   Develop a plan for checking on yourself at the end of the thirty day period. Here are some suggestions.
   - Ask your friend to quiz you on how you are progressing.
   - Write a reminder on your calendar so that you will notice it at the end of thirty days.
5. Keep At It

   Remember that worthwhile goals sometimes take a long time to achieve. And there will be obstacles. Consider them an inevitable and keep working on your goals.

CHAPTER 8

SHARING: We're All in This Together

Confess your faults one to another, and pray for one another, that ye may be healed.
—*James 5:16*

The structured experiences on the following pages are for use by groups of 10 to 15 persons and a leader. Such groups may be:

- A church group that is already formed.
- Several persons in a neighborhood or community "club" who wish to engage in structured growth experiences.
- A group of adults on a week-end retreat.
- College or university classes on human potential.

Each experience is designed to last approximately one hour, with the exception of the last two sessions, which may take more than one hour to complete in a satisfactory manner.

The structured experiences are written as directions to a leader. However, the nature of the directions involves all group members in participation.

To encourage this participation, the leader should arrange the room so that members may face each other. A semicircle of chairs or chairs around a large table is suggested. Also, the room should be large enough for members to move around or work in several small groups.

The following general rules should be followed as the group moves through the experiences. You may wish to write these rules on a chart and post them in the room so that group members can be reminded of them frequently.

- Each member should share openly with other members, but no member should be persuaded to share more than he really wishes to share.
- Each member should affirm the other members' thoughts, feelings, and actions, but affirmation should be given only in sincerity. Feedback should be honest.
- Each member should practice the art of listening, not only for the words but also for the meanings the other persons seek to convey.
- Each member should assume that he can enrich his own life and the lives of others through sharing in these experiences.

Session 1: Getting Acquainted

Purpose: To help participants become acquainted with each other and to deepen mutual appreciation and trust.

Preparation: Secure the following material: A 12″ by 20″ sheet of poster board, a 3-foot piece of string, and a felt-tip marker for each participant.

Procedure: Give each participant one of each of the above materials. Ask the participants to take ten minutes to draw a symbol that they may use to introduce themselves to the other participants. Don't assume that members already know each other, even if they have been meeting together for a long time. The symbol may be a caricature; a pie with various slices representing different aspects of life; a series of words; a life-line; or other symbols that group members create.

Ask the participants to attach the string to two corners of the poster board so they can hang the poster around their necks. Allow each participant to share his symbol with other members of the group.

Session 2: Examining Values

Purpose: To help participants examine their primary values and commit themselves to becoming growing persons.

Preparation: Have on hand a number of magazines and newspapers.

Procedure: Take a few minutes at the beginning of the session to suggest that much of the modern advertising is based upon the selling of a product that appeals to the values held by the consumer. Then ask the participants to thumb through the magazines or papers to determine what each ad is suggesting about a value in the life of the consumer. If time permits, provide paste, scissors, and sheets of newsprint, and ask the participants to make a collage of some of the values they think the average person holds. Then ask class members to share their conclusions with the group. Ask, which of these values contribute to our growth as Christian persons? Which values hinder our growth? List these values in two columns on a chalkboard, placing the positive values in one column and the negative values in the other. Number each column consecutively. Then give each member a sheet of paper and ask him to list the positive and negative values that he believes are operative in his life. Ask him to write a paragraph at the bottom of the paper indicating how he needs to change his value system to achieve more Christian growth. As time permits, allow participants to share what they have written in a voluntary and spontaneous manner.

Session 3: Sharing Histories

Purpose: To help participants gain insight into how their pasts have influenced their present living patterns.

Preparation: No special preparation needed.

Procedure: Ask each participant to relate a personal experience from his past that has influenced him to be the way he is now. The experience may be from childhood, adolescence, or adulthood. It may be religious or secular, joyful or painful.

Then ask the participants to break into pairs. Each person should repeat to the other person's satisfaction what he heard the other person say, including not only the words, but his perception of the feelings behind the words. Allow fifteen or twenty minutes for this process. Then reassemble the participants into one group. Reflect upon what happened in the process. How did each member feel sharing personal data? What was learned through sharing and feedback?

Session 4: Sharing Hopes

Purpose: To help participants gain insight into how their concept of the future affects their present living.

Preparation: Secure from a drug store small prescription containers equal to the number of participants. In advance, duplicate copies of the assignment described below and place one in each container.

Procedure: Give each participant a container in which the following assignment is contained:

Think thirty years ahead. You have just finished writing your autobiography. If you think you will not be alive thirty years from now, assume that someone has just finished writing your biography. Such writings usually try to sum up the outstanding characteristics of the person, the effects of his life. Write a summary of what you would like to be included in that writing. Be ready to share your summary with the group and to explore the following questions: (1) Why do I think I will be alive or dead thirty years from now? (2) In what way is my concept of the future influencing my life now?

After the participants have completed the assignment, lead them to share their hopes with the group. Also, lead the group to explore with each member his answers to the two questions included in the assignment.

Session 5: Assuming Responsibility

Purpose: To help participants discover the extent to which they assume responsibility for their being.

Preparation: Prepare copies of the following test for each participant.

Procedure: Give each participant a copy of the following test.

Responsibility Inventory [1]

This inventory is designed to help you get a realistic picture of the degree to which you accept responsibility for yourself. The only "right" answer is the one that genuinely describes you as you really are now. Don't pretend to be better or worse than you think you are. The only purpose is to help you in your growth.

Read each item and decide how it describes you. Answer by placing in the blank in Column A in front of each number:

+ + if it is very much like you
+ if it tends to be like you
0 if you can't decide
— if it tends to be not like you
— — if it is very much unlike you

Column A (As I am now)	Column B (Desire to change)	Item Number
____	____	1. I am a responsible person.
____	____	2. I fear that I will fail when I try new things.
____	____	3. When people insist, I give in.
____	____	4. I can usually make up my mind and stick to it.
____	____	5. My decisions are not my own.
____	____	6. I often feel helpless.
____	____	7. I can't seem to make up my mind, one way or the other.
____	____	8. I seldom worry about something once I have done it.
____	____	9. I often find myself doing what I don't want to do and neglecting what I want to do.
____	____	10. I am self-reliant.

Now read over each item again and decide whether, if you could, you would like to change in this particular characteristic. If you are satisfied, place a 0 in Column B. If you wish to change, place an X in Column B.

Be prepared to share your conclusions with the group.

Session 6: Examining Self-concepts

Purpose: To help group members get in touch with their self-concepts.

Preparation: Have on hand pennies, dimes, quarters, half-dollars, and dollar bills equal to the number of participants.

Procedure: Place the coins in the middle of the room. If a table is used, place them in the middle of the table. Ask each person to select a coin that represents how he feels about himself. Then ask him to explain why he chose the coin. After each person gives his explanation, ask other participants to choose from the pile of coins, a coin that represents what they consider the person to be worth, give him the coin, and tell why he chose that coin for him.

Session 7: Relating to Others

Purpose: To help group members discover people to whom they relate in a comfortable manner and explore ways to expand their circle of relationships.

Preparation: Duplicate copies of the assignment. Provide paper and pencil.

Procedure: Give each member a copy of the following assignment:

Assume that you have to spend the rest of your life on a remote island with just six people and no one else. Imagine that! None of these six people can be anyone you already know, but you are allowed to specify what they should be like. What kinds of people would you pick to live the rest of your life with? You might think about how old they would be, their sex, the things they would like to do, and the things they would not like to do, their personalities, their looks, or any other qualities. Assume, also, that all your basic needs are taken care of, so you don't have to scrounge around for food, clothing, and shelter. All you have to do is describe as fully as you can what the people you would choose to live with would be like.[2]

- Who would you include?
- Who would you not include?
- What do your choices teach you about how you relate to other people? In what ways are your conclusions consistent with the teachings of Jesus? In what ways do they differ?

Allow about fifteen minutes for participants to complete the activity. Then call for them to share their conclusions with the group.

Session 8: Tending to the Self

Purpose: To help participants explore ways to deal with negative emotions.

Preparation: Make advanced assignments to four people who will report as described below.

Procedure: Call on four people who have studied chapter 4 to report as follows:

- Why do people feel tense?
- Why do people feel depressed?
- Why do people feel guilty?
- Why are people afraid?

Then divide the participants into four groups of equal size. Ask them to discuss the content of the reports in terms of their own personal experience.

Session 9: Investing the Self

Purpose: To help participants explore the extent that they grow through giving themselves to worthwhile endeavors.

Preparation: No special preparation required.

Procedure: Explain that there will be three exploration groups in this session. Participants may choose the one they wish to join. If all participants want to explore the same topic, allow them to do so. You may wish to give equal time to all three topics. The topics to be discussed are as follows. There are no special rules, only the general rules that apply to all sessions.

- How my job helps or hinders my growth.
- How family members help or hinder my growth.
- How I grow through helping other people. How other

people help me.

Session 10: Understanding God

Purpose: To help participants examine their concept of God and their relationship to him.

Preparation: Have on hand a number of copies of old magazines and newspapers, newsprint, paste, and scissors.

Procedure: Give each participant three magazines or newspapers. Ask him to make a collage that represents God as he perceives him. Then call on each participant to show his collage and interpret it. Assign one group member to ask each participant, "Is your view of God consistent with the God revealed in the Bible?" In what ways?"

Session 11: Nurturing the Spiritual Life

Purpose: To help participants develop motivation and skills in motivating and nurturing their spiritual lives.

Preparation: No special preparation required.

Procedure: On the chalkboard, write the following statements.

- I pray when . . .
- The things I pray about most are . . .
- I knew my prayer was answered when . . .
- My greatest hindrance to prayer is . . .
- I use my Bible . . .
- My church helps me to . . .

Ask the participants to discuss these questions by sharing their personal experiences related to them.

Session 12: Sharing Goals

Purpose: To lead participants to establish and share goals for Christian growth.

Preparation: Duplicate sheet described below. Provide

pencils.

Procedure: Give each participant a sheet of paper on which the following questions are written. Leave room between the questions for them to write. (1) What goals for personal Christian growth would you like to achieve in the next year? (2) What do you plan to do to achieve these goals? (3) How can the other participants help you achieve those goals? Allow the participants about twenty minutes to write the goals. Then call on them to share them as time permits. Continue this procedure for the first part of Session 13.

Session 13: Contracting for Mutual Support

Purpose: To lead participants to contract with each other to provide support for personal Christian growth.

Preparation: No special preparation required.

Procedure: Continue the sharing of goals constructed in Session 12. When all participants have shared their goals, lead in a discussion of ways the participants may support each other in achieving their goals. Possible ways include:

- Planning to meet at some future time to check progress
- Telephoning each other to offer encouragement
- Praying for each other
- Suggesting resources to help each other

Close the session with special prayer for the growth of each person in Christian personhood.

NOTES

Chapter 1

1. Lewis Joseph Sherrill, *Struggle of the Soul* (New York: The Macmillan Company, 1959), p. 6.
2. A. H. Maslow, *The Farther Reaches of Human Nature* (New York: The Viking Press, 1971), pp. 25-26.
3. J. Winston Pearce, *The Window Sill of Heaven* (Nashville: Broadman Press, 1958), p. 103.

Chapter 2

1. I am indebted to David Riesman, et al., *The Lonely Crowd,* for the terminology of radar people and gyroscope people. The discussion of the characteristics are my interpretation and differ to some degree from theirs.
2. Robert Bretall, ed., *A Kierkegaard Anthology* (Princeton, 1946), p. 285.

Chapter 3

1. Margaret Craven, *I Heard the Owl Call My Name* (New York: Dell Publishing Company, 1973) p. 9.
2. Milton Mayeroff, *On Caring* (New York: Harper and Row, Publishers, 1971), p. 2.

3. Maslow, *op. cit.*, p. 49.

4. From *Proclaim*, July—September, 1973. Copyright, 1973. The Sunday School Board of the Southern Baptist Convention.

5. From *Review and Expositor*, January, 1960, p. 10.

6. From *The Real Self* (A series of cassette tapes published and copyrighted by Human Development Institutes, Chicago, 1973).

7. From *On Listening* (a cassette tape published and copyrighted by Human Development Institute, Chicago, 1971).

Chapter 4

1. *The Sickness unto Death*, trans. Walter Lowrie (New York: Doubleday and Company, 1954), p. 155.

2. Pearce, *op. cit.*, pp. 75-76.

3. H. C. Brown, Jr., *Walking Toward Your Fear* (Nashville: Broadman Press, 1972).

4. Stanley Rachman, *The Meanings of Fear* (Baltimore: Penguin Books, 1974), p. 66.

5. Granger Westburg, *Good Grief* (Philadelphia: Fortress Press, 1962).

Chapter 5

1. Frank Goble, *The Third Force* (New York: Grossman Publishers, 1970).

2. Wayne E. Oates, *Confessions of a Workaholic* (Nashville: Abingdon Press, 1972), p. 4.

3. I am indebted to Joseph Hinkle, Family Life Section, Church Administration Department, Sunday School Board of the Southern Baptist Convention for much of the information related to present trends in family life.

4. W. O. Thomason, *The Life Givers* (Nashville: Broadman Press, 1972), p. 121.

Chapter 6

1. Robert Wuthnow and Charles Y. Glock, "The Shifting Focus of Faith," *Psychology Today*, November, 1974, pp. 131-58.

Chapter 7

1. Milton Mayeroff, *On Caring* (New York: Harper and Row, Publishers, 1971), p. 2.
2. William H. Mikesell, *The Power of High Purpose* (Anderson, Indiana: The Warner Press, 1961), p. 20.
3. Maslow, *op. cit.*, pp. 35-36.

Chapter 8

1. Gerald Wienstein and Mario D. Fantini, *Toward Humanistic Education* (New York: Praeger Publishers, 1970), pp. 123-24.
2. Adapted from *Leading Groups in Personal Growth* by Jackie M. Smith (Richmond: John Knox Press, 1973), pp. 108-11.

Basic Growth Library

FRANKL, VICTOR. *Man's Search for Meaning.* New York, Washington Square Press, Inc., 1963. An excellent "beginner book" on the primacy of meaning in life.

FROMM, ERICH. *The Art of Loving.* New York, Harper and Row, Publishers, 1956. A clear analysis of what it means to love self and others.

GOBLE, FRANK. *The Third Force.* New York, Simon and Schuster, Inc., 1971. A compilation of the extensive works of Abraham Maslow. The focus on human potential provides encouragement and challenge to the reader.

GREENBERG, SAMUEL I. *Neurosis Is a Painful Style of Living.* New York, Signet Books, 1971. If Maslow is correct in his assumption that "neurosis is the failure of personal growth," this small book describes the results of that failure. Practical suggestions for dealing with neuroses are also provided.

JAMES, MURIEL and JONGEWARD, DOROTHY. *Born to Win.* Reading, Massachusetts, Addison-Wesley Publishing Company, 1971. A practical guide to the development of a wholesome self-concept.

MASLOW, ABRAHAM. *The Farther Reaches of Human Nature.* New York, Viking Press, 1971. Encouraging insight and research on the potential of persons.

MAY, ROLLO. *Man's Search for Himself.* New York, W. W. Norton and Company, Inc., 1953. Help for finding the center of strength in life and growing in personhood.

ROGERS, CARL. *A Therapist's View of Personal Goals.* Wallingford, Pa., 1959. Explicit directions for developing goals for growth in personhood.

SCHULTZ, WILLIAM C. *Joy: Expanding Human Awareness.* New York, Grove Press, Inc., 1967. A popular guide to better personal functioning and deeper human relationships.